重庆市普通高中精品选修课程

CHARMING WANSHENG

魅 力 万 盛

主　编　胡淑英　黄险峰　郑洪燊

副主编　陆　艳　罗　娜　何　巧
　　　　王　倩　范泪涛　赵　娟

西南财经大学出版社

中国·成都

图书在版编目(CIP)数据

魅力万盛=Charming Wansheng/胡淑英,黄险峰,
郑洪燊主编;陆艳等副主编.—成都:西南财经大学
出版社,2024.8. --ISBN 978-7-5504-6379-0

Ⅰ.G634.413

中国版本图书馆 CIP 数据核字第 202429VH79 号

Charming Wansheng **魅力万盛**

Meili Wansheng

主　编　胡淑英　黄险峰　郑洪燊
副主编　陆　艳　罗　娜　何　巧　王　倩　范泪涛　赵　娟

策划编辑:李邓超
责任编辑:李建蓉
责任校对:王甜甜
封面设计:张姗姗　墨创文化
责任印制:朱曼丽

出版发行	西南财经大学出版社(四川省成都市光华村街 55 号)
网　　址	http://cbs.swufe.edu.cn
电子邮件	bookcj@swufe.edu.cn
邮政编码	610074
电　　话	028-87353785
照　　排	四川胜翔数码印务设计有限公司
印　　刷	成都市金雅迪彩色印刷有限公司
成品尺寸	170 mm×240 mm
印　　张	8.625
字　　数	156 千字
版　　次	2024 年 8 月第 1 版
印　　次	2024 年 8 月第 1 次印刷
印　　数	1—2000 册
书　　号	ISBN 978-7-5504-6379-0
定　　价	35.00 元

Preface
前言

　　本书是根据《普通高中英语课程标准》的要求和我校英语教学的实际情况与特色，由我校优秀的英语教师团队自主创新编著的英语特色校本选修教材。

　　本教材共分为四个单元，分别以万盛的自然风光、活力旅游、文化底蕴和特色美食为主题，选取贴近学生学习和生活的具有家乡特色的素材，以便于教师进行情境教学和提高学生的学习兴趣。本教材在每一个教学篇目后均附有生词和短语、课文注解、课文译文和家庭作业板块，以便教师在教学中使用和检查学生学习情况，起到为专业课服务的作用。

　　本教材以万盛全域旅游英语为载体，引导学生在心存爱家爱国情怀的同时传承万盛文化瑰宝，致力于提高学生的文化审美能力和鉴赏能力，加强学生的英语知识积淀，夯实学生的英语运用功底，提高学生的英语表达能力，提升学生的英语素养，用传统的爱家德育方法铺就高中学生综合素养的基石。同时，依托本教材开设相关课程是为了融合必修课程和选修课程的优势，积极探索选修课程开发本土化、内容优质化和教学多元化，从而充分发挥选修课的潜在功能。

总之，本教材在内容上体现了实用性、本土性、兴趣性、创新性、实效性和知识拓展性等特点；在形式上对每个教学篇目都做了解析，便于教师开展更有效的、更灵活多样的课堂活动，激发学生的学习兴趣，让他们愉快学习；在教学效果上做到了强化学生的英语功底，传承本地传统文化。

本教材虽经多次修改，但编者能力有限，不足之处在所难免，敬请读者批评指正。

本教材编委会

2024 年 4 月

Contents
目录

Overview　概览

UNIT 1　Natural Scenery　自然风光

UNIT 4　Delicious Food　特色美食

Overview

概览

Lesson 1   Welcome to Wansheng

Wansheng District is located in the south of Chongqing and is at the border of south Chongqing and north Guizhou Province, approximately 70 kilometers to the central urban area of Chongqing and can be reached by car within one hour. It covers an area of 566 square kilometers, including 8 towns and 2 streets with a total population of 240 000. It was under the jurisdiction of Zhenzhou (an administrative region in Tang Dynasty) in AD 642. Wansheng has a history of nearly 1 400 years. It was formerly named as Nantong Mining District in 1955 and renamed as Wansheng District in 1993. It was established as Wansheng Economic and Technological Development Zone in 2011 (hereafter "Wansheng District" for short), governed by Chongqing Municipal Committee and the Municipal Government. With its profound cultural heritage and unique ethnic customs, Wansheng is like a pearl along "the Three Gorges Outer Ring Tourism Line" in the south of Chongqing.

Wansheng is a city in transition. Wansheng began to extract coal on a large scale from 1938. Its coal output once accounted for one quarter of the whole Sichuan's and a half of the whole Chongqing's coal production after the founding of the People's Republic of China, making a significant contribution to the coal, iron and steel industry of Chongqing and even the whole China. In 2009, Wansheng was listed among the second batch of resource-exhausted cities in China and now has achieved preliminary outcomes in transformation. The output of coal mining industry accounts for 5% of the total industrial output value, dropping from 72%, the highest level in history. The regional economy changes from "underground" to "on the ground", "black" to "green" and "single" to "variety". Wansheng was awarded as one of the 7 excellent cities in the 2017 National Transformation Performance Assessment of Resource-Exhausted Cities.

As a tourist district, Wansheng has 22 scenic spots, such as Black Valley and Longlin Stone Forest (a national 5A scenic area), Ordovician Geological Park, Golden Beach, Qingshan Lake National Wetland Park, Mushroom Park and so on. Wansheng is China's favorable tourist district, the national health city, the national leisure agriculture and rural tourism demonstration district, the national pilot district of tourism reform and innovation and the only national pilot district of resource-based city's tourism transformation and development. Wansheng is promoting the development of all-area tourism, and speeding up the construction of national model area for global tourism.

Wansheng is also a district of sports. After more than ten years of exploration, Wansheng has gradually established a new industrial model which now combines the development of cultural tourism with sports. Wansheng is the hometown of badminton and the national reserve base of high-level badminton talents where about 36 famous badminton coaches and athletes like Zhong Bo and Zhang Yawen have been cultivated. Besides, Wansheng is the district in contact with the development of National Fitness Program designed by the State Council, the national demonstration base of sports industry, the first national roller skating training base and the first orienteering training base in China. Wansheng is actively carrying out the national fitness strategy to build a healthy and lively city, and is also speeding up the construction of the national extreme sports base, national sports and health demonstration city, and national sports tourism demonstration district.

（本文图片由万盛发布公众号提供）

Words and expressions 生词和短语

district [ˈdɪstrɪkt] n. 区域；行政区

approximately [əˈprɒksɪmətlɪ] adv. 大约

jurisdiction [ˌdʒʊərɪsˈdɪkʃən] n. 管辖区

administrative [ədˈmɪnɪstrətɪv] adj. 行政的

establish [ɪˈstæblɪʃ] vt. 建立；确立

municipal [mjuːˈnɪsɪpl] adj. 市政的

profound [prəˈfaund] adj. 深远的

heritage [ˈherɪtɪdʒ] n. 遗产

unique [juˈniːk] adj. 独一无二的

ethnic [ˈeθnɪk] adj. 种族的；少数民族的

pearl [pɜːl] n. 珍珠

extract [ikˈstrækt] v. 提取；提炼

transition [trænˈziʃn] n. 转变；过渡

significant [sɪgˈnɪfɪkənt] adj. 显著的

preliminary ［prɪˈlɪmɪnərɪ］ *adj.* 初步的

contact ［ˈkɒntækt］ *n.* 交往；联系

the State Council 国务院

orienteer ［ˌɔːrɪenˈtɪə(r)］ *vi.* 进行定向赛跑

speed ［spiːd］ *n.* 速度　*vi.* 快速行进

demonstration ［ˌdemənˈstreɪʃn］ *n.* 示范

Notes to the texts　课文注解

1. Wansheng District is located in the south of Chongqing. 万盛位于重庆南部。

此句中，be located in 意为"位于，坐落于"，相当于"lie in"。例如：Chongqing is located in / lies in the southwest of China. 重庆位于中国西南部。

2. It covers an area of 566 square kilometers. 万盛占地 566 平方千米。

此句中，cover an area of 意为"占地面积"。例如：It covers an area of 566 square kilometers. 它占地 566 平方千米。

3. The output of coal mining industry accounts for 5% of the total industrial output value. 煤炭采掘业产值占工业总产值的 5%。

此句中，account for 意为"解释；占……比例"。例如：People who are in favor of the idea account for 45%。支持这个主意的人占 45%。

Translation of the reading texts　课文译文

走进万盛

万盛（经济技术开发区）位于重庆南部，地处渝黔边界，距重庆主城 70 千米，1 小时车程即可到达。万盛面积 566 平方千米，辖 8 镇 2 街，总人口 24 万。万盛在唐贞观十六年（642 年）属溱州，至今有近 1 400 年建制史。1955年设立南桐矿区，1993年更名为"万盛区"，2011年设立万盛经济技术开发区（以下不加区别，简称"万盛区"），由重庆市委、市政府直接管理。它以深厚的人文底蕴和独特的民族风情，成为重庆之南、"三峡外环旅游线"上的一颗璀璨明珠。

万盛是一座转型城市。万盛于1938年开始大规模采煤，曾被誉为"抗战煤都"。中华人民共和国成立后，其煤炭产量一度占四川的1/4、重庆的1/2，为重庆乃至国家煤炭、钢铁工业作出了重大贡献。万盛产业发展长期"一煤独大"，2009年被列入全国资源枯竭型城市，目前转型取得初步成效：煤炭采掘业产值占工业总产值的比重由历史最高72%下降到5%，地区经济实现从"地下到地上、黑色到绿色、单一到多元"的转变，2017年，万盛在资源枯竭型城市转型绩效考核中获评全国7个优秀城市之一。

万盛是一座旅游城市，拥有5A级景区黑山谷·龙鳞石海和奥陶纪国家地质公园、板辽湖金沙滩、青山湖国家湿地公园、蘑菇总动员等22个景区景点，是中国优秀旅游城市、国家卫生城市、全国休闲农业与乡村旅游示范区、国家级旅游业改革创新先行区、全国唯一的国家资源型城市旅游转型发展试点区，正在推进全域旅游发展，加快建设国家全域旅游示范区。

万盛是一座体育城市。经过10年的探索，万盛逐渐形成了一种旅游业和体育业相结合的产业模式。万盛是羽毛球之乡，也是国家羽毛球高水平体育后备人才基地，先后培养输送了钟波、张亚雯等36名知名羽毛球教练员和运动员。万盛是国务院"全民健身计划"研制工作联系城市、国家体育产业示范基地、全国首个全项目轮滑赛训基地、全国首个定向运动训练基地，正在推进全民健身国家战略的实践，打造活力之城、健康万盛，加快建设全国极限运动基地、全国全民运动健康模范城市、全国体育旅游示范区。

Homework 家庭作业

Answer the questions and give a brief introduction of Wansheng in not more than 100 words.

1. Where is Wansheng located?

2. How much land does Wansheng cover?

3. What reasons led to Wansheng's transition?

UNIT 1　Natural Scenery

自然风光

Lesson 2
The Introduction to Black Valley

A city of mountains and rivers, a beautiful place! Lively Wansheng of All-Area Tourism!

Wansheng, 70 kilometers away from the main city of Chongqing, can be reached in one hour by car. The scenery of Wansheng is magnificent, among which Black Valley is the most famous.

Black Valley, a national 5A scenic spot, lies in Heishan Town, Wansheng Economic Development Zone, Chongqing, 20 kilometers away from Wansheng city. The total length of the scenic spot is 13 kilometers. The main landscape is "one island, three valleys, five gorges, seven districts, twelve peaks, thirty-six bridges, ninety-nine waterfalls, and one hundred and eight ponds". Black Valley is regarded as a paradise on the earth for sightseeing.

With few people, high mountains, and dense forests, it preserves the intact natural ecology of a few subtropical and temperate zones at the same latitude on the earth. At present, it is the largest natural ecological scenic spot in Chongqing. It is also the first scenic spot in China to set ecological health standards.

In Black Valley, there are various rare animals and plants. Because its forest coverage rate is 97% and the concentration of negative oxygen ions is as high as 110 000 per cubic centimeter, Black Valley is also known as "the most beautiful health care valley in China" as well as "Chongqing and Guizhou Biological Gene Bank".

(本文图片由万盛旅游提供)

Words and expressions　生词和短语

Black Valley 黑山谷

tourism [ˈtʊərɪzəm] n. 旅游业

gorge [gɔːdʒ] n. 谷，峡谷

Outer Ring 外环

scenery [ˈsiːnərɪ] n. 风景

magnificent [mæɡˈnɪfɪsənt] adj. 雄伟的

scenic spot 风景区

Economic Development Zone 经济开发区

length [leŋθ] n. 长度

landscape [ˈlændskeɪp] n. 风景

peak [piːk] n. 山峰

waterfall [ˈwɔːtəfɔːl] n. 瀑布

paradise [ˈpærədaɪs] n. 天堂

sightseeing [ˈsaɪtsiːɪŋ] n. 观光

dense [dens] adj. 稠密的

preserve [prɪˈzɜːv] *v.* 保存

intact [ɪnˈtækt] *adj.* 完好无损的

ecology [iˈkɒlədʒɪ] *n.* 生态

subtropical [ˌsʌbˈtrɒpɪkl] *adj.* 亚热带的

temperate [ˈtempərət] *adj.* 温带的

latitude [ˈlætɪtjuːd] *n.* 维度

at present 目前，现在

set ... standard 设定……的标准

various [ˈveərɪəs] *adj.* 各种各样的

rare [reə(r)] *adj.* 稀少的，稀有的

coverage rate 覆盖率

concentration [ˌkɒnsnˈtreɪʃn] *n.* 浓度

negative oxygen ion 负氧离子

cubic centimeter 立方厘米

gene bank 基因库

Notes to the texts　课文注解

1. The scenery of Wansheng is magnificent, among which Black Valley is the most famous. 万盛的风景雄伟壮观，其中以黑山谷最为出名。

此句中，among which 是"介词+关系代词"，关系代词 which 引导非限定性定语从句，先行词是 scenery，指物。例如：In London, there are many attractions that interest me a lot, among which is Big Ben. 在伦敦，有很多吸引我的名胜，其中一个是大本钟。

2. Black Valley is regarded as a paradise on the earth for sightseeing. 黑山谷被看作观光游览的人间天堂。

此句中，be regarded as 意为"被看作……"。例如：The brave young

man is regarded as a hero for saving the boy's life. 这位勇敢的年轻人被认为是英雄，因为他拯救了男孩的生命。

3. ..., Black Valley is also known as "the most beautiful health care valley in China" as well as "Chongqing and Guizhou Biological Gene Bank". ……黑山谷又被誉为"中国最美养生峡谷"和"渝黔生物基因库"。

此句中，be known as 意为"作为……而出名"。例如：Luxun was known as a writer. 鲁迅是作为一个作家而出名的。

Translation of the reading texts 课文译文

黑山谷简介

山水之城，美丽之地！全域旅游，活力万盛！

万盛，距重庆主城 70 千米，1 小时车程即可到达。万盛的风景雄伟壮观，其中以黑山谷最为出名。

国家 5A 级景区——黑山谷位于重庆市万盛经开区黑山镇，距万盛城区 20 千米。景区全长 13 千米，主要景观为"一岛、三谷、五峡、七区、十二峰、三十六桥、九十九瀑、一百零八潭"。黑山谷被看作观光游览的人间天堂。

这里人迹罕至、山高林密，完好地保存着地球上同纬度为数不多的亚热带和温带自然生态。这里也是目前重庆地区最大的自然生态风景区，是全国首个制定生态健康标准的风景区。

黑山谷里，珍稀动植物种类繁多。因为森林覆盖率达 97%，负氧离子浓度高达 11 万个/立方厘米，黑山谷又被誉为"中国最美养生峡谷"和"渝黔生物基因库"。

Homework　家庭作业

Your friend Alice plans to visit Black Valley and she writes a letter asking for some information about sights there. Please write a brief introduction of Black Valley about 100 words.

Lesson 3   The Beauty of Black Valley

—Beautiful Water

The beauty of Wansheng lies in its winding Black Valley, stacked distant mountains, shrouded mist, continuous valleys and ink wonderland.

Water is the soul of Black Valley. The silky and soft Mengsha Waterfall, the rushing Dragon Waterfall, the magnificent Flying Fish Waterfall, countless hanging springs, flying streams, cliffs and mist form a fresh and distant ink painting.

Mengsha Waterfall

Mengsha Waterfall is the most elegant and beautiful waterfall among the 72 waterfalls in Black Valley. It flows down the cliff slowly and looks graceful across the river, just like a white gauze dancing in the wind. It is like a dream, so it is called Mengsha Waterfall.

Dragon Waterfall

Dragon Waterfall usually has a small amount of water, just like flying flowers and splashing jade. In spring and summer, especially after heavy rains, the waterfall is very spectacular. It is seven or eight meters wide,

hanging in the mountains. The water flows straight down 3 000 *chi*. The sound of water resounds through the whole valley like a roaring dragon with extraordinary power, so it is called Dragon waterfall.

Flying Fish Waterfall

Flying Fish Waterfall is one of the most surprising waterfalls in Black Valley Scenic Spot. The drop is about 80 meters. In the rainy season of summer, the waterflow can reach 5 tons per second. Because of the fish shape, it is named Flying Fish Waterfall.

（本文图片由万盛旅游提供）

Words and expressions　生词和短语

beauty ['bjuːtɪ] *n.* 美丽

lie in 在于

winding ['wɪndɪŋ] *adj.* 蜿蜒的

stack [stæk] *v.* 使……成叠

distant ['dɪstənt] *adj.* 遥远的

shroud [ʃraʊd] *v.* 隐藏，遮盖

mist [mɪst] *n.* 薄雾

continuous [kən'tɪnjuəs] *adj.* 连续的

wonderland ['wʌndələænd] *n.* 仙境

soul [səʊl] *n.* 灵魂

silky ['sɪlkɪ] *adj.* 如丝绸一样的

Mengsha Waterfall 梦纱瀑

Dragon Waterfall 神龙瀑

magnificent [mæɡˈnɪfɪsnt] *adj.* 宏伟的

Flying Fish Waterfall 飞鱼瀑

countless [ˈkaʊntləs] *adj.* 无数的

cliff [klɪf] *n.* 峭壁

form [fɔːm] *v.* 形成

elegant [ˈelɪɡənt] *adj.* 优雅的

graceful [ˈɡreɪsfl] *adj.* 优美的

gauze [ɡɔːz] *n.* 薄纱

amount [əˈmaʊnt] *n.* 数量

splash [splæʃ] *v.* 泼洒

jade [dʒeɪd] *n.* 玉，翡翠

spectacular [spekˈtækjələr] *adj.* 壮观的

straight [streɪt] *adv.* 径直地

resound [rɪˈzaʊnd] *v.* 回荡

roar [rɔː(r)] *v.* 吼叫，咆哮

extraordinary [ɪkˈstrɔːdənərɪ] *adj.* 非凡的

water flow 流量

Notes to the texts　课文注解

1. The beauty of Wansheng lies in its winding Black Valley, stacked distant mountains, shrouded mist, continuous valleys and ink wonderland. 万盛之美，美在黑山幽谷，远山层叠，薄雾笼罩，峡谷连绵，水墨仙境。

此句中，lie in 意为"位于/在于……"。例如：The car accident lied in his carelessness. 这次车祸在于他的粗心。

2. It is like a dream, so it is called Mengsha Waterfall. 它如梦似幻，故

名梦纱瀑。

此句中，be called 意为"被叫作……"。例如：The little boy is called Tom. 这个小男孩被叫作 Tom。

3. It is seven or eight meters wide, hanging in the mountains. 瀑布有七八米宽，挂在山间。

此句中，hanging 是现在分词作状语，与句子主语是主动关系，意为"挂在……"。例如：The woman is sitting on the grass, reading a book. 这个女人坐在草坪上看书。

4. Flying Fish Waterfall is one of the most surprising waterfalls in Black Valley Scenic Spot. 飞鱼瀑是黑山谷景区最令人惊叹的瀑布之一。

此句中，one of + 形容词最高级+可数名词复数，意为"最……之一"。例如：Chongqing is one of the most beautiful cities in China. 在中国，重庆是最美丽的城市之一。

Translation of the reading texts 课文译文

黑山谷之美

秀水

万盛之美，美在黑山幽谷，远山层叠，薄雾笼罩，峡谷连绵，水墨仙境。

水是黑山谷的灵魂。如丝如缕的梦纱瀑，急浪若奔的神龙瀑，气势磅礴的飞鱼瀑，以及数不清的悬泉、飞流、绝壁、烟霭，构成一幅清新淡雅的水墨画。

梦纱瀑

梦纱瀑是黑山谷 72 瀑中最雅致、最漂亮的瀑布。它沿着崖壁缓缓流下，隔河望去，婀娜多姿，宛如一袭白纱，随风轻舞。它如梦似幻，故名梦纱瀑。

神龙瀑

神龙瀑平时水量较小，如飞花溅玉；春夏时节，大雨过后，瀑布就非常壮观。瀑布有七八米宽，挂在山间。飞流直下三千尺，那水声，响彻整个峡谷，犹如神龙长啸，气势非凡，故名神龙瀑。

飞鱼瀑

飞鱼瀑是黑山谷景区最令人惊叹的瀑布之一。其落差约 80 米，夏天雨季，水流量可达五吨/秒。因瀑布的形态似鱼，故名飞鱼瀑。

Homework　家庭作业

Answer the questions：

1. How many waterfalls are mentioned in this text?

2. Can you describe these waterfalls in this text?

Lesson 4   The Green of Black Valley

−*Green Gorge*

In Black Valley, the spiritual mountains, beautiful water, dense forests, ancient and green gorges, high and towering cliffs, wonderful streams and flying waterfalls, flowing water and deep pools, cool wind and clean oxygen, floating bridges, suspension bridges and plank roads are all vividly impressed in my mind, which makes me feel that no other gorge can be equal to it after enjoying through this gorge.

Dragon Gorge

Dragon Gorge is 1 200 meters long with thousands of twists and turns. The winding path is like a snake. The narrowest part is only 2 meters and the widest part is less than 30 meters. On both banks, there are many stacked mountains, strange rocks, thousands of cliffs, many flowing rocks and continuous waterfalls. It is named after the Dragon Spring, which is the only tribute spring in the ancient Yelang Country.

Jinji Gorge

Jinji Gorge has a "V" shape gorge with a total length of 360 meters and a vertical height of nearly 500 meters. The rock walls on both sides are stacked one

after another, the mountains are magnificent and steep, the current is rushing, and the peaks are inserted into the sky. In the bamboo thicket of the valley, in addition to the amazing flowers and plants, there is often a unique bird species in China—the famous red belly bird just for watching at home and abroad. Therefore, it is named Jinjin Gorge.

Black Monkey Gorge

The total length of Black Monkey Gorge is 420 meters, and the narrowest part is only 2 meters. The dangerous peaks on both sides overlap and interlock, and the bank wall tilts more than 90 degrees. You can hardly see the sun all the year. Even in the middle of summer, when the sun is shining, the air is cool. Black Monkey Valley gets its name because of Francois langur—a national first-class protected animal, which often climbs, jumps and plays here.

（本文图片由万盛旅游提供）

Words and expressions　生词和短语

spiritual ['spɪrɪtʃuəl] *adj.* 灵魂的
dense [dens] *adj.* 浓密的
towering ['tauərɪŋ] *adj.* 高耸的
stream [striːm] *n.* 小溪

oxygen [ˈɒksɪdʒən] n. 氧气

floating bridge 浮桥

suspension bridge 吊桥

plank road 栈道

vividly [ˈvɪvɪdlɪ] adv. 栩栩如生地

impress [ɪmˈpres] v. 给……留下印象

Dragon Gorge 神龙峡

twists and turns 迂回曲折

winding [ˈwɪndɪŋ] adj. 蜿蜒的

narrow [ˈnærəʊ] adj. 狭窄的

stack [stæk] v. 使……层叠

name after 以……命名

tribute [ˈtrɪbjuːt] n. 贡品

Jinji Gorge 锦鸡峡

total [ˈtəʊtl] adj. 全部的

vertical [ˈvɜːtɪkl] adj. 垂直的

height [haɪt] n. 高度

steep [stiːp] adj. 陡峭的

current [ˈkʌrənt] n. 水流

insert [ɪnˈsɜːt] v. 嵌入

thicket [ˈθɪkɪt] n. 灌木丛

in addition to 除……之外，还……

amazing [əˈmeɪzɪŋ] adj. 令人惊叹的

unique [juˈniːk] adj. 独一无二的

red belly bird 红腹锦鸡

at home and abroad 国内外

Black Monkey Gorge 黑猴峡

overlap [ˌəʊvəˈlæp] *v.* 重叠

tilt [tɪlt] *v.* 倾斜

degree [dɪˈɡriː] *n.* 度数

Francois langur 黑叶猴

Notes to the texts　课文注解

1. ..., which makes me feel that no other gorge can be equal to it after enjoying through this gorge. 这一切都让我感觉到，游过此峡之后，再没有其他的峡谷能与之媲美了。

此句中，which 引导非限定性定语从句，在从句中作主语，指代前面整个句子。例如：Mary passed the important exam, which made her parents very happy. 玛丽通过了这个重要的考试，这让她的父母非常高兴。

2. Dragon Gorge is 1 200 meters long with thousands of twists and turns. 神龙峡全长 1 200 米，峡谷千曲百折。

此句中，with 是介词，意为"有……"。例如：Jinji Gorge has a "V" shape gorge with a total length of 360 meters and a vertical height of nearly 500 meters. 锦鸡峡呈"V"形，全长 360 米，垂直高度近 500 米。

3. It is named after the Dragon Spring, which is the only tribute spring in the ancient Yelang Country. 其因沟内有被视为古夜郎国唯一贡泉的"神龙泉"而得名。

此句中，name after 意为"以……名字命名"。例如：The school is named after that famous professor. 这所学校是以那位著名教授的名字命名的。

4. In the bamboo thicket of the valley, in addition to the amazing flowers and plants, there is often a unique bird species in China... 在峡谷内的竹灌丛中，除有令人叹绝的奇花异草外，常有中国特有鸟种……

此句中，in addition to 意为"除……以外，还……"。例如：In addition to my studies, I take part in a lot of interesting activities. 除了学习以外，我还参加许多有趣的活动。

Translation of the reading texts　课文译文

黑山谷之绿
——碧峡

黑山谷的灵山、秀水、密林、古朴幽深的碧峡、高耸对峙的峭壁、美溪飞瀑、流泉深潭、凉风清氧、浮桥、吊桥、栈道，这一切都让我感觉到，游过此峡之后，再没有其他的峡谷能与之媲美了。

神龙峡

神龙峡全长 1 200 米，峡谷千曲百折，曲径如走蛇，最窄处只有 2 米，最宽处近 30 米。两岸群山层峦叠嶂，怪石嶙峋，峭壁千仞，岩多流纹，飞瀑不断。其因沟内有被视为古夜郎国唯一贡泉的"神龙泉"而得名。

锦鸡峡

锦鸡峡呈"V"形，全长 360 米，垂直高度近 500 米。两侧岩壁层层叠叠，山势雄奇险峻，水流奔腾湍急，夹岸峰插云天。在峡谷内的竹灌丛中，除有令人叹绝的奇花异草外，常有中国特有鸟种、驰名中外的观赏鸟——红腹锦鸡出没，因此得名"锦鸡峡"。

黑猴峡

黑猴峡全长 420 米，最窄处仅 2 米宽。两崖险峰重叠，犬牙交错，崖壁倾斜超过 90 度，长年累月难见天日。即使在烈日高照、炎热难耐的盛夏，这里也是凉风嗖嗖、寒气袭人。其因有国家一级保护动物黑叶猴经常攀跳、嬉戏于此而得名。

Homework 家庭作业

Answer the questions：

1. What is the main idea of this text?

2. How many gorges are mentioned in this text?

3. What are characteristics of these gorges in this text?

Lesson 5   The Fun of Black Valley

—*Floating Bridge*

In Black Valley, there are all kinds of bridges: trestle bridge, suspension bridge, floating bridge, corridor bridge, stone arch bridge, stone pier bridge, swinging and shaking bridge, giving visitors a thrilling and exciting experience.

Visitors are walking on the suspension bridges and floating bridges, moving forward through the bumps. Among them, the most interesting one is the exciting floating bridge where visitors walk just like roaming in the Dragon Palace.

The floating bridges in Black Valley are very distinctive. They are set up on the Liyu River at the border of Chongqing and Guizhou. There is no obvious border between them. The tourists sway between the two regions, which is very exciting.

The left and right ends of the bridge are respectively marked by Chongqing and Guizhou. Standing on the bridge and stepping on two regions at the same time, people feel heroic. It is said that people standing in the narrowest Liyu Gorge can touch the mountains of Chongqing with one hand and the mountains of Guizhou with the other hand.

By the connection of these bridges over the Liyu River, people shuttle between Chongqing and Guizhou from the left bank to the right. It is they that witness the bustle between Chongqing and Guizhou.

（本文图片由万盛旅游提供）

Words and expressions 生词和短语

floating bridge 浮桥

trestle bridge 栈桥

suspension bridge 吊桥

corridor bridge 廊桥

stone arch bridge 石拱桥

stone pier bridge 石墩桥

swinging and shaking bridge 灯晃桥

thrilling [ˈθrɪlɪŋ] *adj.* 惊险的

move forward 前进

bump [bʌmp] *n.* 碰撞

roam [rəʊm] *v.* 徜徉，漫步

Dragon Palace 龙宫

distinctive [dɪˈstɪŋktɪv] *adj.* 独特的

border [ˈbɔːdə(r)] *n.* 边境

obvious [ˈɒbviəs] *adj.* 明显的

sway [sweɪ] *v.* 摇摆

province [ˈprɒvɪns] *n.* 省

respectively [rɪˈspektɪvlɪ] *adv.* 各自地

heroic [həˈrəʊɪk] *adj.* 英勇的

shuttle ['ʃʌtl] *v.* 频繁往来

witness ['wɪtnəs] *v.* 见证

bustle ['bʌsl] *n.* 喧嚣

Notes to the texts　课文注解

1. Among them, the most interesting one is the exciting floating bridge where visitors walk just like roaming in the Dragon Palace. 其中，最为有趣的就是这紧张刺激的浮桥，游人步行在浮桥上，如在龙宫漫游。

此句中，where 引导定语从句，在从句中作地点状语，修饰 bridge。例如：We visited the factory where your father worked last year. 我们去参观了你父亲去年工作的那个工厂。

2. Standing on the bridge and stepping on two regions at the same time, people feel heroic. 站在桥上，同时踏两省市，让人顿生豪迈之感。

此句中，standing 是现在分词作状语，表主动。例如：Crossing the street, we should be careful. 过马路时，我们应该小心。

3. It is said that people standing in the narrowest Liyu Gorge can touch the mountains of Chongqing with one hand and the mountains of Guizhou with the other hand. 据说人站在最窄的鲤鱼峡中，一只手可摸到重庆的山，另一只手则可摸到贵州的山。

"It is said that +从句" 中，it 作形式主语，意为"据说……"。例如：It is said that all of us passed the exam. 据说，我们所有人都通过了这次考试。

4. It is they that witness the bustle between Chongqing and Guizhou. 也正是他们，见证着渝黔边界的喧嚣。

此句中，It is... that... 为强调句型，意为"正是……"。例如：It is the young man that often gives us some help. 正是那个年轻人经常给我们一些帮助。

Translation of the reading texts 课文译文

黑山谷之趣
——浮桥

在黑山谷里，散布着各式各样的桥：栈桥、吊桥、浮桥、廊桥、石拱桥、石墩桥、灯晃桥，步步惊心。

游人在这一座座的吊桥和浮桥上行走，在颠簸摇晃间前行。其中，最为有趣的就是令人紧张刺激的浮桥。游人步行在浮桥上，如在龙宫漫游。

黑山谷的浮桥非常有特色，它们架设在重庆和贵州交界的鲤鱼河上，没有明显的分界，游人在两省市之间摇来晃去的，非常刺激。

桥的左右两端分别标识重庆和贵州。站在桥上，同时脚踏两省市，让人顿生豪迈之感。据说人站在最窄的鲤鱼峡中，一只手可摸到重庆的山，另一只手则可摸到贵州的山。

在鲤鱼河上，靠着这些桥的连接，人们忽而左岸忽而右岸，在重庆和贵州之间穿梭往返。也正是他们，见证着渝黔边界的喧嚣。

Homework 家庭作业

Answer the questions:

1. Which kinds of bridges are there in Black Valley?

2. When the visitors are walking on the floating bridge, what are their feelings?

3. Where are these floating bridges set up?

4. What are the functions of these floating bridges?

Lesson 6   The Function of Black Valley

—Biological Gene Bank

It was another sunny day after the rain. Cheng Kepeng, a staff member of Black Valley Scenic Spot, walked into the Black Monkey Gorge of Black Valley with apples, bananas and other fruits. Cheng Kepeng said Black Monkey Gorge was named because Francois langurs often hang out here. The fruit in his hand was given for them to eat. Why did Cheng Kepeng want to "get close to" Francois langur?

"Francois langur is the image ambassador of Black Valley." Cheng Kepeng introduced. It is a national first-class protected animal with a body length of about 50 centimeters, a small head and a long tail. It is dark all over, with a  pinch of upright black crown hair on its head and a white hair on both sides of its cheeks. It is very cute.

Why can Francois langurs appear in Black Valley? Some people say it is because of its beautiful scenery and good air. It turns out that because Black Valley is located on the border of Chongqing and Guizhou, it is inaccessible and conserves a lot of forest resources, with a forest coverage rate as high as 97%. Up to now, more than 1 800 species of plants and 300 kinds of vertebrates have been discovered.

It is understood that apart from Francois langur, there are also various

national first-class and second-class protected animals and plants in Black Valley. At the same time, four national first-class protected plants and all kinds of national second-class protected plants were found in Black Valley.

Visitors often wonder why so many rare animals and plants live and grow in Black Valley.

"Only a few areas with unique geographical environment have not been attacked by glaciers and have become havens for life." Cheng Kepeng introduced, "Black Valley is such a safe haven." Black Valley is not only a witness to the vicissitudes of life, but also a shelter for rare plants. Therefore, it is also known as "Chongqing Guizhou Biological Gene Bank".

（本文图片由万盛旅游提供）

Words and expressions　生词和短语

staff ［stɑːf］ *n.* 职员

Francois langur 黑叶猴

hang out 闲逛

image ambassador 形象大使

a pinch of 一小撮……

upright ［ˈʌpraɪt］ *adj.* 直立的

crown ［kraʊn］ *n.* 皇冠

turn out 结果是……

locate ［ləʊˈkeɪt］ *v.* 确定……的位置

inaccessible ［ˌɪnækˈsesəbl］ *adj.* 难以达到的

conserve ［kən'sɜːv］ *v.* 保存

as high as 高达

up to now 直到现在

vertebrate ［'vɜːtɪbrət］ *n.* 脊椎动物

apart from 除此以外，而且……

various ［'veəriəs］ *adj.* 各种各样的

geographical ［ˌdʒiːə'ɡræfɪkl］ *adj.* 地理学的

attack ［ə'tæk］ *v.* 攻击

glacier ［'ɡlæsiə(r)］ *n.* 冰川

haven ［'heɪvn］ *n.* 避风港

vicissitude ［vɪ'sɪsɪtjuːd］ *n.* 变迁

shelter ［'ʃeltə(r)］ *n.* 避难所

Notes to the texts　课文注解

1. It turns out that because Black Valley is located on the border of Chongqing and Guizhou, it is inaccessible and conserves a lot of forest resources, with a forest coverage rate as high as 97%. 原来，黑山谷由于地处重庆和贵州边界，人迹罕至，保存了大量森林资源，森林覆盖率高达 97%。

在 "It turns out that + 从句" 中，it 作形式主语，意为 "原来……"。例如：It turns out that the tickets have been sold up. 原来，票已经卖完了。

此句中，be located on 意为 "位于……（河流）上"。例如：Chongqing is located on the Yangtze River. 重庆位于长江之上。

2. Up to now, more than 1 800 species of plants and 300 kinds of vertebrates have been discovered. 到现在为止，1 800 多种植物和 300 多种脊椎动物已被发现。

此句中，up to now 意为"到现在为止"，要与现在完成时连用。例如：Up to now, we have learned 3 000 English words. 到现在为止，我们已经学习了 3 000 个英文单词。

3. It is understood that apart from Francois langur, there are also various national first-class and second-class protected animals and plants in Black Valley. 据了解，除了黑叶猴，黑山谷还有种类繁多的国家一级和二级保护动植物。

此句中，It is understood that... 意为"据了解……"。例如：It is understood that all of us passed the exam. 据了解，我们所有人都通过了考试。

Translation of the reading texts　课文译文

黑山谷之用
——生物基因库

又是一个雨过天晴的日子，黑山谷景区工作人员成克鹏提着苹果和香蕉等水果走进黑山谷黑猴峡。成克鹏说，黑猴峡是因为此处经常有黑叶猴出没而得名，他手中的水果是送给黑叶猴吃的。成克鹏为啥要与黑叶猴"套近乎"呢？

"黑叶猴是黑山谷的形象大使。"成克鹏介绍道。它是国家一级保护动物，体长大约 50 厘米，头小尾长，全身漆黑，头顶有一撮直立的黑色冠毛，面颊两边各有一道白毛，非常可爱。

黑叶猴为啥能出现在黑山谷呢？有人说，因为黑山谷山清水秀，空气好。原来，黑山谷由于地处重庆和贵州边界，人迹罕至，保存了大量森林资源，森林覆盖率高达 97%。到现在为止，1 800 多种植物和 300 多种脊椎动物已被发现。

据了解，除了黑叶猴，黑山谷还有种类繁多的国家一级和二级保护动植物。同时，有四种国家一级保护植物和多种国家二级保护植物在黑山谷被发现。游客常常不解：黑山谷为什么居住和生长着这么多珍稀动植物？

"只有少数地理环境独特的地区没有受到冰川的袭击，成为生物的避风港。"成克鹏介绍道，"黑山谷就是这样一个避风港。"黑山谷既是沧海桑田的见证者，也是珍稀植物的避难所。因此，黑山谷又被誉为"渝黔生物基因库"。

Homework　家庭作业

Answer the questions：

1. Can you describe the black monkeys in Black Valley?

2. What can we do to protect Black Valley–Biological Gene Bank?

Lesson 7   The Natural Scenery of Longlin Stone Forest

Longlin Stone Forest is an extraordinary national geological park. It is a typical karst landform. We can appreciate many kinds of grotesque caves and fancy rocks there.

Tianmen Cave

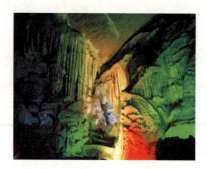

Tianmen Cave is a typical karst cave. The tough limestones in the cave are presenting thousands of postures after being scoured and corroded by the underground water for hundreds of millions of years. You may appreciate various karst landscapes, including clint, tor, stalactite, underground river, etc. in the cave and experience the miracle of great nature. What is the most strange and particular is the "dormant window" in the middle of the cave. The "dormant window" was formed as the ceiling of the rock gradually fell due to corrosion, and tourists can see the sun, the moon and the stars through the "window". Tianmen Cave is thereby named.

Galloping Stone Horses

These strange and various stones just look like galloping war-horses, showing an overwhelming force. This scenic spot is one of the best scenic spots in the Longlin Stone Forest. When you are there, it seems as if you entered an ancient battlefield filled with clouds of smoke, floating over.

A Swath of Sky

This is a typical karst ravine shaped by running water for millions of years. If the cliffs on both sides are cut, you will find they are all made up of huge stones with similar sizes and shapes, weighing dozens of tons, just like the artificial ancient city walls. You will feel overwhelmed when walking through them. There are three sights of this kind in the Longlin Stone Forest. The largest, longest and most beautiful one is about 300 meters long, from the starting point to the ending point, while the width is between 1 and 2 meters, and the deepest is about 50 meters. When walking through the two cliffs towering into the sky, one may feel that he comes to an ancient age. Looking up at the sky, you can only see a swath of sky.

Fan-Shaped Stone

The fan, 6 meters high, 6.5 meters in diameter, and the thinnest part less than 0.5 meter, spreads in north and south direction. The 200-ton fan-shaped stone, standing firmly on a stone column less than 1 meter in diameter, has won a name of "the Biggest Fan of the World". Strangely, in hot summer days, as long as people approach the stone fan, they will feel the cool wind and feel refreshed.

Stone Towers Forest

There stand various shapes of stone towers, high and low, with no one identical. Some are dangerous and steep, some simple and solemn, some smart and elegant, while some high and magnificent.

Sinoceras

Sinoceras, i.e. Orthoceras, only living in the Ordovician ocean, is a typical fossil in Longlin Stone Forest. It was named as "Sinoceras Fossil" by experts. Orthoceras, literally meaning "straight horn", generally 15 centi-

meters long, existed 460 million years ago. Around its mouth are about ten wrists on which there are many small suckers. Once small animals touch the suckers, they will be sucked and then swallowed.

Fossil Gallery

The total length of the fossil gallery is about 50 meters, which was formed in the Ordovician period 440 million years ago. The biggest difference between Longlin Stone Forest, Yunnan Stone Forest and Sichuan Stone Forest is that there are no fossils or few fossils in the other two places. However, there are many kinds and forms of fossils such as stone turtles, stone shells, stone snails, stone eggs and so on here. The majority of them are the hornstones formed in Cambrian, most of which are yellowish brown. Some are exposed on the surface of the stone, while others are embedded in the stone with grotesque postures.

Censer-Like Peak

It's a censer-shaped mountain with randomly arranged stones and winding roads. Climbing up the mountain, you may have an overview of the Longlin Stone Forest. Especially when the rain is over and the weather is clear, clouds and mist are mixed. It is just like a fairyland. There, you can hear the roar of the waterfall down the mountain. The Censer-Like Peak is special not only because of its beautiful appearance, but also because it is a geomantic treasure. The villagers of Miao family regard it as a holy mountain, and they will go to the mountain to worship Buddha to wish a good harvest and happiness every year. Therefore, the incense on the Censer-Like Peak keeps burning all the year round, adding her mysterious color.

Lovers Stone

Lovers Stone is a scenic spot formed by karst landform, consisting of a pair of stones, which are the symbol of firm love. Couple stones are divided into male and female. The two stones are very lifelike in shape, just like a pair of lovers hugging each other tightly, with a meaning of staying forever. The south part is like a muscular man, while the north part is like a graceful woman. People coming here often place the red knots before the stones to pray for a firm love.

Besides the above grotesque caves and fancy rocks, there are many other scenic spots you can't miss in Longlin Stone Forest.

（本文图片由万盛发布公众号提供）

Words and expressions　生词和短语

kast landform 喀斯特地貌

appreciate ［əˈpriːʃiˌeɪt］ vt. 了解；欣赏

limestone ［ˈlaɪmˌstəʊn］ n. 石灰岩

scoure ［ˈskaʊə］ vt. 冲洗；冲刷

corrode ［kəˈrəʊd］ vt. （逐渐）削弱，侵蚀

clint ［klɪnt］ n.【地】石芽

tor ［tɔː］ n. 崎岖的高山；石山

galloping [ˈɡæləpɪŋ] *adj.* 疾驰的；飞奔的

stalactite [ˈstæləktaɪt] *n.* 钟乳石

swath [swɔːθ] *n.* （长）条；细长的列

ravine [rəˈviːn] *n.* （流水冲刷而成的）沟壑

refreshed [rɪˈfreʃt] *adj.* 新鲜的；恢复活力的

magnificent [mæɡˈnɪfɪsənt] *adj.* 壮观的

wrist [rɪst] *n.* 腕；腕关节

suck [sʌk] *vt.* 吸食；吸入

swallow [ˈswɒləʊ] *vt.* 吞下；咽下

Cambrian [ˈkæmbriən] *n.* 【地】寒武纪

expose [iksˈpəuz] *v.* 暴露

be exposed to 暴露在

embed [imˈbed] *vt.* 埋入；嵌于

censer-like peak 香炉峰

tenderness [ˈtendənɪs] *n.* 柔和；柔美

geomantic [dʒɪəˈmæntɪk] *adj.* 风水的

incense [ˈɪnsens] *n.* 香；香味

Notes to the texts　课文注解

1. What is the most peculiar is the "dormant window" in the middle of the cave. 最奇特的是中间的天窗。

此句中，what is the most peculiar 是一个由 what 引导的主语从句。

2. When walking through the two cliffs towering into the sky, one may feel that he comes to an ancient age. 穿行其间，犹如步入远古隧道。

此句中，when walking through the two cliffs towering into the sky 可看作一个省略句，省略了共同的主语 one，以及谓语动词 is。

3. Climbing up the mountain，you may have an overview of Longlin Stone Forest. 登临远眺，整个龙鳞石海尽收眼底。

此句中，climbing up the mountain 是一个分词短语，作时间状语，表示主动。

4. 震旦角石

别名：中华角石

拉丁文学名：Sinoceras

生存年代：中奥陶世（4.75亿年至4.6亿年前）

震旦角石是海生无脊椎软体动物化石，隶属于头足纲塔飞角石目、喇叭角石科、震旦角石属，常见于我国南部中奥陶纪地层中。

震旦角石具有坚硬的外壳，壳体或直或盘卷，壳体表面有波状横纹，壳内有很多横板，壳长可达二米以上，多数在几十厘米至一米之间。当纵向剖开时，可以看见其指向壳尖端细长锥状的体管；而在横切面中心，可以看见其圆形的体管。体管与壳体直径相比较小，大多位于接近中央的地方，有的接近边缘。震旦角石化石长度最长可达一米多，一般在二十至六十厘米之间。保存完整、构造清晰的震旦角石，以及波状横纹和体管较为清晰者、体型较人较长且未缺失尖端者，通常具有较高的科研、收藏和观赏价值。同时震旦角石也是我国《古生物化石保护条例》保护、管理的化石之一，可见其珍贵性。

Translation of the reading texts 课文译文

龙鳞石海之自然景观

龙鳞石海景区是一个国家地质公园，属于典型的喀斯特地貌景观。我们可以在这里看到奇形怪状的岩洞和岩石。

天门洞

天门洞是典型的喀斯特溶洞地貌。

经过地下水数亿年的溶蚀和冲刷，坚硬的石灰岩被雕琢得千姿百态，可谓鬼斧神工。洞内石芽、石山、钟乳、地下河等岩溶景观丰富，令人目不暇接，不禁感叹大自然的奇妙。最奇特之处在洞的中部，因顶部岩石逐渐溶蚀塌落，从而形成“天窗”。游客在洞内便可直接观赏日月星辰，天门洞也由此而得名。

万马奔腾

错落有致、光怪陆离的巍巍巨石，犹如万千扬蹄疾奔的骏马，其势恢宏壮观、势不可挡，观之犹闻战马萧萧长鸣，不绝于耳，令人叹为观止。当你身临其中时，犹如你已经进入一个硝烟弥漫的古战场。

一线天

典型的地缝溶洞地貌，经亿年流水冲刷而成。两边悬崖若削，你会发现整个石崖均由大小形状相似、重达数十吨的巨石块组成，犹如人工铸成的古城墙一般。穿行其间，大有目不暇接之感。这样的一线天在龙鳞石海中有三条。其中最大、最长、最美的一条从起点到终点长约 300 米，而宽则在 1 米到 2 米之间，最深的有 50 米左右。穿行其间，犹如步入远古隧道。仰望长空，蓝天仅存一线。

石扇

扇面呈南北向，高 6 米，直径 6.5 米，最薄处不足 0.5 米。重 200 吨的石扇矗立在直径不足 1 米的石柱上，数亿年牢固如常，享有“天下第一扇”的盛名。奇怪的是，炎炎夏日，人们只要一走近石扇，便会感到凉风习习，神清气爽。

千塔林

石塔高低错落，姿态万千，无一雷同。有的险峻峭拔；有的古朴庄重；有的小巧别致，顾盼多姿；有的高大雄伟，傲视苍穹。

震旦角石

震旦角石学名直角石，是生活在奥陶纪海洋中的特有动物，为龙鳞石海景区的代表性化石，被专家命名为“中华震旦角石化石”。直角石的字面含义为"笔直的角",体长一般 15 厘米,生存年代为 4.75 亿年至 4.6 亿年前,嘴巴四周长有十条左右的腕,腕的腹面有许多小吸盘,小动物一经接触,就被它吸住吞食。

化石长廊

化石长廊全长约 50 米,形成于 4.4 亿年前的奥陶纪。万盛龙鳞石海与云南石林和四川石海最大的区别是,其他两个地方没有化石或化石稀少。而万盛龙鳞石海化石种类繁多,形态各异,诸如石龟、石贝壳、石螺、石蛋等。最多的是形成于寒武纪的角石,它们大多呈黄褐色,有的露在石头的表面,有的镶嵌于石头中,其姿态千奇百怪。

香炉峰

该山峰因形似香炉而得名。山石错落,曲折蜿蜒。登临远眺,整片龙鳞石海尽收眼底,特别是雨过天晴的时候,云雾缭绕,恰似仙境。身处香炉山,可以听山下瀑布倾泻而下的轰鸣声。

香炉山的奇特不仅在于它的美丽,而且在于它是一块风水宝地。苗家的父老乡亲把它视为一座神山,在喜获丰收或喜庆节日都会到香炉山,上香拜佛,以祈求他们年年都五谷丰登、幸福吉祥。所以香炉山上常年香火不断,更增添了它的神秘色彩。

情侣石

这是由喀斯特地貌形成的景点,由一对石头组成,这对石头是坚贞不渝的爱情的象征。情侣石是有雌雄之分的,两块石头形态非常逼真,就像一对痴情男女紧紧拥抱在一起,有一种入心的缠绵之意。南面这块就像是肌肉发达的男子,而北面的这块就像一位身材曼妙的女郎。来这儿的人们经常会放红色的中国结在情侣石前,以祈求一段坚贞的爱情。

除了以上千姿百态的岩石和岩洞以外,龙鳞石海景区还有很多你不可错过的景点。

Homework   家庭作业

What's the effect tourism has brought to Wansheng? How to protect Longlin Stone Forest from being destroyed? Think about the questions carefully and write your answers on the exercise book.

Lesson 8   The Human Landscape of Longlin Stone Forest

Shilin Town of Wansheng is a place where the Miao minority mainly live. So you can experience the culture of Miao minority with Wansheng's local characteristics here.

Miao Palace

Miao Palace is a new scenic spot which is designed and built according to the style of the Miao family. People can appreciate the architectural style of Miao minority and experience Miao culture.

Peach Blossom Ground

There are many scenic spots in Peach Blossom Ground, such as Peach Blossom Pond, Peach Blossom Ditch, Wishing Stone and so on. It is said that the quiet and romantic Peach Blossom Ground is a place for young men and women of Miao minority to date and make wishes. When the peach blossoms are in full bloom, lovers will admire the moon and sing the love songs here. They will also make a wish of eternal love under the peach trees, facing the everlasting stone forest.

Stone Drum Square

The bucket drum, also known as the "hanging drum", is one of the major percussion instruments of the Miao minority. It is generally 70 to 80 centimeters long, with the diameter of 40 to 50 centimeters, and is made of cow leather and bamboo nails. The Miao people believe that everything has spirit. They often worship the nature and their ancestors on the Stone Drum Square. In the worshiping activities, bucket drums are the must-have instruments.

Miaolongling

Miaolongling, part of Longlin Stone Forest, is said to be a holy place where people of Miao Nationality worship nature and pray for blessings. Standing there, people can have a full view of Longlin Stone Forest.

The Sucked Home Brew House

The sucked home brew is a unique traditional drink of the Miao people. The production process of it is very exquisite. The Sucked Home Brew House is for manually brewing wine. When holding important activities, people will drink the sucked home brew made by themselves.

Liu Qianshun's Tomb

The ancient tomb with exquisite workmanship and unique design is of Liu Qianshun's, a priest in Daoguang Years of Qing Dynasty. There are four Chinese characters "Liu Shi Jia Cheng" on the top of the tomb. A pair of stone lions on the left and right represent the power of the owner. There are many laughers in front of the tomb, representing the wealth of the Liu family. The golden ducks next to it stand for the geomantic omen here. The carved double dragons grabbing beads, follow the traditional saying that Chinese people are the descendants of dragons. It's said that Liu's ancestors in three generations were all officers and were popular with the common people.

The Sedan Songs

The sedan song was edited by the sedan bearers of Shilin to coordinate the movements of the front and back of the sedan. These sedan songs coming from life reflect the wisdom of the sedan owners. The sedan songs sound very interesting and are easy to sing. For example, when the bearer in the front sees water on the ground, he will shout "The sun is shining" to remind the bearer at the back. The bearer at the back will reply "There is standing water on the ground", so he would be very careful. When there is a turning head, the bearer in the front will sing "winding winding ahead" and the bearer at the back will reply "walking walking slowly". The sedan bearers act in cooperation to make sure the safety of both visitors and the sedan bearers themselves.

（本文图片由万盛发布公众号提供）

Words and expressions   生词和短语

the Miao minority 苗族

exquisite [ɪkˈskwɪzɪt] *adj.* 精美的

guard [gɑrd] *vt.* 守护；防御

eternal [ɪˈtɜːnl] *adj.* 永恒的；不变的

troop [truːp] *n.* 军队；一群

bucket [ˈbʌkɪt] *n.* 水桶；吊桶

percussion [pəˈkʌʃ(ə)n] *n.* 撞击；震动

instrument [ˈɪnstrəmənt] *n.* 用具；乐器

worship [ˈwɜːʃɪp] *vt.* 崇拜   *n.* 礼拜

sedan [sɪˈdæn] *n.* 轿车；轿子

sedan bearer 轿夫

cooperation [kəʊˌɒpəˈreɪʃn] *n.* 合作；协作

priest [priːst] *n.* 牧师；教士

Notes to the texts   课文注解

1. The bucket drum, also known as the "hanging drum", is one of the major percussion instruments of the Miao minority. 万盛苗族的打击乐器主要为桶鼓，也称"吊鼓"。

此句中，known as the "hanging drum" 是过去分词短语，作后置定语。
be known as... 意为"作为……而闻名"。

2. Miaolongling, part of Longlin Stone Forest, is said to be a holy place where people of Miao minority worship nature and pray for blessings. 苗龙岭，龙鳞石海著名景点之一。据传，苗龙岭是古时苗族崇拜自然、焚香烧纸、祭祀祈福之地。

此句中，part of Longlin Stone Forest 是 Miaolongling 的同位语。where people of Miao minority worship nature and pray for blessings 是一个由 where 引导的定语从句，修饰 place。此句可以替换为：It is said that Miaolongling, part of Longlin Stone Forest, is a holy place where people of Miao minority worship nature and pray for blessings.

Translation of the reading texts 课文译文

龙鳞石海之人文景观

万盛石林镇是辖区内苗族主要居住地。因此，在这儿，你就可以体验具有万盛地方特色的苗族的文化。

苗王宫

苗王宫，是按照苗家风貌设计打造的新景点。在这里，可以欣赏到苗族的建筑，体验苗族的文化。

桃花坞

桃花坞有桃花潭、桃花沟、海枯石烂、许愿石等景点。相传幽静浪漫的桃花坞，是苗族青年男女相会许愿之地。

每逢桃花盛开，有情人携手相约在花前树下，面对亿年恒久的石林，谈情说爱，对歌赏月，共同祈福终生。

石鼓广场

万盛苗族的打击乐器主要为桶鼓，也称"吊鼓"。桶鼓一般长 70~80

厘米，直径40~50厘米，用牛皮蒙面、竹钉钉制而成。苗族信奉万物有灵，他们经常在石鼓广场崇拜自然、祀奉祖先。而在祭祀活动中，桶鼓是必备的乐器。

苗龙岭

苗龙岭，是龙鳞石海著名景点之一。据传，苗龙岭是古时苗族崇拜自然、焚香烧纸、祭祀祈福之地。站在这里，几乎可以看到整个龙鳞石海景区。

咂酒坊

咂酒是苗族人特有的一种传统饮品，其制作工艺十分考究，咂酒坊就是他们的手工酿酒作坊。当举行重大活动时，他们会喝自己酿造的咂酒。

刘公墓

古墓做工精细，设计别致，坐相讲究。墓的主人刘乾顺，是清道光年间的一位道台。墓的上方有"刘氏佳城"四个大字。其左右有一对石狮子，左大右小，代表墓的主人的权利。墓前方有许多笑人头，代表刘家家财万贯。旁边的金鸭子代表这里的风水。墓上所雕刻的双龙抢珠，沿袭了中国人是龙的传人的传统说法。据说刘家祖上三代为官，积德行善，福泽一方，深受百姓拥戴。

轿歌

轿歌是石林轿夫们为使抬轿的前后两人动作协调而自编的。这些源于生活的轿歌体现了轿夫们的聪明才智。轿歌唱起来朗朗上口，听起来极有情趣。比如前面的轿夫看见地上有水，为提醒后面的轿夫，他喊"天上明晃晃"，后面的轿夫应一声"地上水凼凼"，并格外小心。前方有转弯时，前面的轿夫喊"弯弯头"，后面的轿夫应"慢慢走"。轿歌的前呼后应，确保了轿夫和游客的安全。

Homework 家庭作业

Find more information about the Miao minority and share it with classmates next class.

Lesson 9   Qingshan Lake National Wetland Park

The beauty of Wansheng lies in its mountains at dusk. Surrounded by mountains and lakes, Wansheng shows its grateful elegance reflected in the blue waves and ripples. Qingshan Lake National Wetland Park, surrounded by green mountains, has a vast expanse of water, dotted with islands and harbors. When the sun sets at dusk, the lake surface is sparkling with ripples, presenting a wonderful pastoral scenery.

The scenic spot covers an area of about 2 200 hectares, 8 kilometers from Wansheng town. There are various types of wetlands and abundant resources in the scenic spot, with diverse landscapes such as lakes, peninsulas, waterfalls, streams, ditches, valleys, bays, ponds, forests and mountains. Among them, Spring Scenery of Pear Garden, Mountains at Dusk, Fragrance of Autumn Os-

manthus, Health Waterfall, Foggy Villages and Water Woods are the most famous landscapes. They show the wonderful blend of the natural landscape and the ecological environment. The scenic spot also con-

tains national intangible cultural heritage Ensemble of Wind and Percussion Instruments of Jinqiao, patriotism education bases such as Ziru Cemetery, clifftombs in Eastern Han Dynasty and other special tourist spots. In the scenic spot, there are also recreational facilities for fishing, barbecue, water cruise, real-sense shooting, archery and even a professional RV camp.

Of all the landscapes in the scenic spot, Health Waterfall is the most remarkable one. Formerly known as Liushuiyan Waterfall, it is located in the Lake Bay across from the Liu-shuiyan Bridge. In front of Health Waterfall, there is a cliff about 100 meters wide and 40 meters high in the Lake Bay, which is surrounded by dense

bamboo and wood. A running waterfall with a height of 10 meters comes down from the mountain top, which is so spectacular. With green mountains faintly undulating and the water flowing all the way, it's an ideal paradise for everybody.

There tourists can escape from the city, and be away from the prosperity, enjoying the leisure time in the green mountains and waters. Walking on the fitness trail around the lake which is more than 100 miles long, you can enjoy the beautiful scenery, take exercise, as well as experience the happiness brought by the combination of exercise and travel.

（本文图片由万盛发布公众号提供）

Words and expressions　生词和短语

elegance ['elɪgəns] *n.* 优雅，雅致

ripple ['rɪpl] *n.* 波纹；涟漪

dot [dɒt] *v.* 加点；散布于，遍布

sparkling ['spɑːrklɪŋ] *adj.* 闪闪发光的

pastoral ['pæstərəl] *adj.* 田园生活的

hectare ['hekter] *n.* 公顷（等于 1 万平方米）

abundant [ə'bʌndənt] *adj.* 丰富的；充裕的

peninsula [pə'nɪnsələ] *n.* 半岛

osmanthus [ɒz'mænθəs] *n.* 桂花

landscape ['lændskeɪp] *n.* 风景

blend [blend] *n.* 混合；混合物

intangible [ɪn'tændʒəbl] *adj.* 无形的

heritage ['herɪtɪdʒ] *n.* 遗产；传统

cemetery ['semətərɪ] 陵园

cliff-tomb 崖墓

patriotism ['peɪtrɪətɪzəm] *n.* 爱国主义

recreational [ˌrekrɪ'eɪʃənl] *adj.* 娱乐的

facility [fə'sɪlətɪ] *n.* 设施，设备

archery［ˈɑːtʃərɪ］n. 射箭；箭术

RV 房车

faintly［ˈfeɪntlɪ］adv. 微弱地；模糊地

undulating［ˈʌndʒəleɪtɪŋ］adj. 波浪起伏的

paradise［ˈpærədaɪs］n. 天堂

prosperity［prɒˈsperətɪ］n. 繁荣

trail［treɪl］n. 小道

combination［ˌkɒmbɪˈneɪʃn］n. 结合体

Notes to the texts 课文注解

1. There are various types of wetlands and abundant resources in the scenic spot, with diverse landscapes such as lakes, peninsulas, waterfalls, streams, ditches, valleys, bays, ponds, forests and mountains. 景区湿地类型多样，湿地资源丰富，拥有湖、半岛、瀑布、溪、沟、谷、湾、塘、林、山等多样化景观。

其中 various types of 意为 "不同种类的" "各种各样的"，相当于 different kinds of, all kinds/ sorts of。例如：There are various types of the disease. 该疾病有各种类型。

2. The scenic spot also contains national intangible cultural heritage Ensemble of Wind and Percussion Instruments of Jinqiao, patriotism education bases such as Ziru Cemetery, cliff-tombs in Eastern Han Dynasty and other special tourist spots. 景区内还拥有国家级非物质文化遗产金桥吹打、爱国主义教育基地子如陵园、东汉崖墓群等特色旅游点。

其中 Ensemble of Wind and Percussion Instruments of Jinqiao 为专有名词，意为金桥吹打，已经申请国家级非物质文化遗产，是当地的一大特色。

3. A running waterfall with a height of 10 meters comes down from the

mountain top, which is so spectacular. 一道飞瀑从数十米高的山头直挂而下，气势壮观。

其中 with a height of 10 meters 为介词短语，作后置定语，修饰 waterfall；which 引导一个非限制性定语从句，补充说明飞瀑气势壮观。

Translation of the reading texts　课文译文

青山湖国家湿地公园

万盛之美，美在青山晚照。依山傍水，大气柔美，碧波荡漾，绮丽多姿。青山湖国家湿地公园，四面青山环抱，延绵起伏，苍翠浓密，水域辽阔。岛屿星罗棋布，港湾纵横交错。傍晚时分，夕阳西沉，晚霞当空，波光粼粼，一派湖光山色、锦绣田园。

景区占地面积约 2 200 公顷，距万盛城区约 8 千米。景区湿地类型多样，湿地资源丰富，拥有湖、半岛、瀑布、溪、沟、谷、湾、塘、林、山等多样化景观。其中，梨园春色、青山晚照、秋月闻桂、养生飞瀑、晴雨烟村、水中林泽为最著名的景观。它们呈现出自然景观与生态环境的极致交融。景区内还有国家级非物质文化遗产金桥吹打、爱国主义教育基地子如陵园、东汉崖墓群等特色旅游点。该景区有垂钓、烧烤、水上游船、实感射击、射箭等游乐设施，并设有专业的房车营地。

在景区所有的景点中，最令人瞩目的当属养生飞瀑。养生飞瀑原名流水岩瀑布，位于流水岩大桥里面的湖湾。在养生飞瀑前的湖湾处，有一个宽约 100 米、高约 40 米的悬崖，四周竹木茂密。一道飞瀑从数十米高的山头直挂而下，气势壮观。青山隐隐起伏，江流千里迢迢。它是每个人理想的世外桃源，可以让人逃离都市，远离繁华，在青山绿水中享受漫漫时光。漫步在 50 余千米长的环湖健身步道上，游客可以欣赏美丽风景，锻炼体魄，尽享体旅结合带来的快乐。

Homework 家庭作业

According to the text and your own experience to Qingshan Lake National Wetland Park, write a composition called "The Beauty of Qingshan Lake National Wetland Park". Please write no more than 120 words.

UNIT 2   Dynamic Travel
活力旅游

Lesson 10   Ordovician Geological Park

—*Fun and More Than Fun*

Ordovician Geological Park is famous for its unique tourist resources, which can date back to the Ordovician Era about 456-600 million years ago. The stone forests and peaks from the Ordovician period are covered with rock vine plants.

It is the magic of nature that gives birth to the world wonder that "in the forest are stones, on which grow trees, so trees and stones coexist together". The stone forest of various forms is hidden in the vegetation, just like lots of natural bonsais, and therefore is also known as "Green Stone Forest". What is particularly amazing is that there are many karst caves, ground crevices and so

on, making it called "Underground Palaces" in Ordovician scenic spot by experts. The unique ornamental, and scientific exploration value, as well as good ecological living environment of the Ordovician scenic spot are extremely rare in surrounding areas of Chongqing.

Ordovician Geological Park is also known as Fantasy Ordovician, for there are a variety of entertainment facilities and modern cinemas as well. More than ten extreme high-altitude activities have been created upon the 300-meter high cliff, such as Sky Hanging Corridor, the thrilling Cliff Swing, and the Cliff Bungee Jumping. Among them, the most famous and breathtaking is Sky Hanging Corridor, under which is the precipitous cliff. The whole hanging corridor is made of transparent glass, stretches out the cliff and hangs in the air, making it so thrilling to walk on. In addition, Sky Hanging Corridor is currently the longest hanging glass corridor in the world, which has set a Guinness World Record.

In a word, not only can you appreciate the naturally formed strange mountains and rocks in the scenic spot, but also experience adventure and excitement. No wonder Ordovician Geological Park is regarded as a must-visit attraction by people. If you want to have fun and more than fun, come to Ordovician Geological Park!

（本文图片由万盛发布公众号提供）

Words and expressions　生词和短语

Ordovician [ˌɔːdəʊˈvɪʃən] *n.* 奥陶系，奥陶纪

era [ˈɪərə] *n.* 时代；年代；纪元

vegetation [ˌvedʒəˈteɪʃn] *n.* 植被；植物

bonsai [ˈbɒnsaɪ] *n.* 盆景；盆景艺术

karst cave 溶洞

crevice [ˈkrevɪs] *n.* 缝隙

ornamental [ˌɔːnəˈment(ə)l] *adj.* 观赏性的

corridor [ˈkɒrɪdɔː(r)] *n.* 走廊

precipitous [prɪˈsɪpɪtəs] *adj.* 险峻的；急躁的

transparent [trænsˈpærənt] *adj.* 透明的

Notes to the texts　课文注解

1. Ordovician Geological Park is famous for its unique tourist resources, which can date back to the Ordovician Era about 456-600 million years ago. 奥陶纪地质公园因其旅游资源独特而闻名，可以追溯到距今 4.56 亿~6 亿年的奥陶纪时代。

其中 date back to 是动词短语，意为"追溯到；从……开始有"。例如：This tradition can date back to ancient times. 这一传统可以追溯到古代。

2. It is the magic of nature that gives birth to the world wonder that "in the forest are stones, on which grow trees, so trees and stones coexist together". 大自然的神奇造化孕育出了这里"林中有石，石上有树，树石共生"的天下奇观。

此句中 it is... that... 为强调句，强调句中又含有一个 that 引导的同位

语从句，修饰 wonder；which 引导一个非限制性定语从句，补充说明 stones；而 in the forest are stones, on which grow trees，为两个完全倒装句型。

give birth to 是动词短语，意为"生（孩子），生育；引起，产生"。例如：The queen gives birth to all the bee children. 蜂后生育了所有的蜜蜂。

3. In a word, not only can you appreciate the naturally formed strange mountains and rocks in the scenic spot, but also experience adventure and excitement. 总之，你不仅能够在奥陶纪景区欣赏到天然形成的奇山怪石，而且能够体验惊险与刺激。

此中 not only..., but also... 为并列连词，连接两个并列的句子，其中 not only 引导的句子进行部分倒装。例如：Not only does she speak Spanish, but also she's good at computers. 她不仅会说西班牙语，还精通计算机。

Translation of the reading texts　课文译文

奥陶纪地质公园
——不只是有趣

奥陶纪地质公园因其旅游资源独特而闻名，其可以追溯到距今 4.56 亿~6 亿年前的奥陶纪时代。奥陶纪时期的石林、石峰上长满了岩藤植物。

大自然的神奇造化孕育出了这里"林中有石，石上有树，树石共生"的天下奇观。其石林形态多样，掩映于植被之中，好似一幅幅天然盆景，被誉为"绿色石林"。尤为奇绝的是整个景区有多处溶洞、地缝等，被专家称为奥陶纪景区的"地下宫殿"。其独特的观赏和科考探险价值、良好的生态人居环境在重庆市周边地区中极为难得。

奥陶纪地质公园也作为梦幻奥陶纪而被大家熟知，因为里面有各种各样的娱乐设施和现代影院。在三百米高的悬崖上，有十多种极端高海拔的活动，如天空悬廊、悬空秋千和悬崖蹦极。其中，最著名和激动人心的就是天空悬廊，它下面就是悬崖峭壁。整个悬廊全部采用透明玻璃搭建而成，其伸出悬崖，吊在半空中，走在上面是如此的惊心动魄。而且，天空悬廊是目前世界上最长的悬挑空中玻璃走廊，创了吉尼斯世界纪录。

　　总之，你不仅能够在奥陶纪景区欣赏到天然形成的奇山怪石，而且能够体验惊险与刺激。难怪奥陶纪地质公园被人们看作一个必游之地。如果你想要玩得开心，并且收获更多，就来奥陶纪地质公园吧！

Homework　家庭作业

Our school "English Weekly" needs a passage about travelling. Please write a travel journal or an introduction to talk about Ordovician Geological Park within 120 words.

Lesson 11　The Youngextreme World

−*A Must-Go Destination for Young Group*

The beauty of Wansheng lies in the Youngextreme World. Sports tourism is vibrant and full of youthful vigor.

The Youngextreme World is next to the north gate of Black Valley in Wansheng, a national 5A scenic spot, covering an area of about 54 acres. Based on the three-dimensional integration of land sports, water sports and air sports, the Youngextreme World is the first sports theme park of this kind in China. The project includes a professional F3 track, off-road vehicle track, the longest karting track in the city, barbecue tent campsite, assembly lawn, water world and so on. Since the Youngextreme World opened in 2017, nearly 100 race track events have been held here, making it a gathering place for racing and sports car enthusiasts in the Southwest. In the Youngextreme World, there is also Ferris wheel, hot air balloon, motorboat, shuffle-board, squash, shooting, e-sports, VR (virtual reality), large

area of trampoline, children's amusement park and other entertainment projects. The Youngextreme World is designed for young groups, integrating fashion, leisure, outdoor expand training, racing events, outdoor performing and so on. In a word, it is a comprehensive teaching and experience tourism scenic spot.

The Youngextreme World offers visitors "a flat-rate package" for well-managed tour throughout the holiday. The first professional racing track in Chongqing, the first AI unmanned aerial vehicle in Southwest China, nearly 30 competitive recreational sports, as well as the master light and shadow show are all set in place to bring visitors exciting moments of vitality and fashion, making it a must-go destination for young group!

（本文图片由万盛发布公众号提供）

Words and expressions 生词和短语

vibrant [ˈvaɪbrənt] *adj.* 充满生机的

three-dimensional integration 三维一体

karting track 卡丁车赛道

assembly [əˈsemblɪ] *n.* 集会，集合

shuffle-board [ˈʃʌflbɔːd] *n.* 沙壶球

squash［skwɒʃ］*n.* 墙网球，壁球

trampoline［ˌtræmpəˈliːn］*n.* 蹦床；弹簧垫

integrate［ˈɪntɪɡreɪt］*vt.* 使成为一体

enthusiast［ɪnˈθjuːzɪˌæst］*n.* 热衷者，狂热者

Ferris wheel 摩天轮

comprehensive［ˌkɑːmprɪˈhensɪv］*adj.* 综合的

flat-rate *n.* 统一价格

Notes to the texts　课文注解

1. Based on the three-dimensional integration of land sports, water sports and air sports, the Youngextreme World is the first sports theme park of this kind in China. 青年汇巅峰乐园基于陆上运动、水上运动、空中运动三维一体，是国内首家以该理念打造的运动主题乐园。

其中 be based on 意为"根据，以……为基础；建立在……基础上"。例如：Your grade will be based on four papers and a final exam. 你的成绩将根据四篇论文和期末考试决定。

2. Since the Youngextreme World opened in 2017, nearly 100 race track events have been held here, making it a gathering place for racing and sports car enthusiasts in the Southwest. 自 2017 年青年汇巅峰乐园开园以来，这里已经举办了近 100 场竞赛，使之成为西南地区赛车和跑车爱好者的聚集地。

其中 since 引导一个时间状语从句，其后主句需用现在完成时态；making it... 为现在分词，作结果状语。

3. The Youngextreme World is designed for young groups, integrating fashion, leisure, outdoor expand training, racing events, outdoor performing and so on. 青年汇巅峰乐园针对年轻群体打造，集时尚、休闲、极限拓展、竞速赛事、户外演艺等于一体。

其中 be designed for 意为"专为……而设计"。例如：The desk of this kind is specially designed for children. 这种书桌是专门为小孩设计的。

Translation of the reading texts   课文译文

青年汇巅峰乐园
——年轻人的必去之地

万盛之美，美在巅峰乐园。体育旅游，青春飞扬。

青年汇巅峰乐园位于万盛国家 5A 级景区黑山谷北门入口旁，占地面积约 54 英亩（1 英亩 ≈ 4 046.86 平方米）。青年汇巅峰乐园基于陆上运动、水上运动、空中运动三维一体，是国内首家以该理念打造的运动主题乐园。其包括专业的 F3 级别赛车道、越野车赛道、本市最长的卡丁车赛道、烧烤帐篷露营地、集会草坪、水上乐园等。自 2017 年青年汇巅峰乐园开园以来，这里已经举办了近 100 场竞赛，成为西南地区赛车和跑车爱好者的聚集地。同时，这里也有摩天轮、热气球、摩托艇、沙壶球、壁球、射击、电子竞技、VR（虚拟现实）、超大面积蹦床、儿童乐园等娱乐项目。青年汇巅峰乐园针对年轻群体打造，集时尚、休闲、极限拓展、竞速赛事、户外演艺等于一体。总之，它是一个综合型教学、体验旅游景区。

青年汇巅峰乐园以"精致一价全包假期"的方式，为游客提供专属旅行管家全程陪伴的度假之旅。重庆首条专业车类赛道、西南首推 AI 无人驾驶飞行器、近 30 个竞技娱乐项目与大师级光影秀，让游客臻享动感时尚，刷新激情梦想。由此，青年汇巅峰乐园成为年轻人的一个必去之地！

Homework　家庭作业

You are Li Hua, and your friend Tom plans to visit the Youngextreme World. Please write an email within 100 words to introduce it to him.

Lesson 12   Banliao Golden Beach

– "The Maldives in Chongqing"

Banliao Golden Beach is an ideal destination for ecological leisure, fashionable sports, amazing recreation and lakeside resort. As the largest inland beach in China, it unrolls a beautiful landscape of winding shores under the blue sky and white clouds, surrounded by undulating mountains covered with tea trees.

Banliao Golden Beach is located in Banliao Village, Youth Town, with quiet and beautiful lake and superior ecological environment. Mountains, lakes, islands, bays, and tea in the scenic spot make it a charming attraction. It is also famous as a water sports base, a leisure fishing center, and a camping destination in Chongqing. There are ten theme activities in the scenic spot, including camping, canoeing, picnic, barbecue buffet, fishing, bonfire carnival, tea making, hiking and mountaineering, Miao family style performance as well as 3D open-air

movies. Among them, Camping Base, Tea Experience Picking Garden, Fishing Center, Kayaking Base and Lotus Garden are so special that many artists come here to do artistic creation and even build art base. More and more tourists from all over the country come here to appreciate the scenery as well as relax on holidays.

Amorous Feelings Beach is the hottest one of all the Banliao Golden Beach scenic spots, with a total area of 132 000 square meters and a beach area of 93 000 square meters. The beach area is flat and open, forming excellent

landscape view. All the sand on the beach is sea sand carried from the seaside far away, with a total of 45 000 tons. The whole beach is divided into three areas, development activity area, leisure activity area and comprehensive activity area. The main entertaining projects include Sunshine Beach, Green Island, Borderless Swimming Pool, Water Flying Man, Motorboats, Frog Croaks from Lotus Pond and so on. With such beautiful beaches and amazing entertaining projects, no wonder Banliao Golden Beach is called "the Maldives in Chongqing".

(本文图片由万盛发布公众号提供)

Words and expressions 生词和短语

destination [ˌdestɪˈneɪʃn] *n.* 目的地，终点
ecological [ˌiːkəˈlɒdʒɪkl] *adj.* 生态的

unroll［ʌnˈrəʊl］*vt.* 展开，铺开；显示

canoeing［kəˈnuːɪŋ］*n.* 皮划艇

bonfire carnival 篝火狂欢

Lotus Garden 荷园

kayaking base 皮艇基地

Amorous Feelings Beach 风情沙滩

croak［krəʊk］*n.* 呱呱叫声

Maldives［ˈmɔːldiːvz］*n.* 马尔代夫

Notes to the texts　课文注解

1. It is also famous as a water sports base, a leisure fishing center, and a camping destination in Chongqing. 它也作为重庆市水上运动基地、重庆市休闲垂钓中心、重庆市露营目的地而闻名。

其中 be famous as 意为"作为……而出名"，后接身份、地位、工作等。注意，be famous for 意为"因……而出名"，后接出名的原因，如特征、性质等。例如：Xiao Zhan is famous as a singer, and is famous for his beautiful songs and charming smiles. 肖战作为一个歌手而出名，他拥有动听的歌声和迷人的微笑。

2. Among them, Camping Base, Tea Experience Picking Garden, Fishing Center, Kayaking Base and Lotus Garden are so special that many artists come here to do artistic creation and even build art base. 其中露营基地、茶叶体验采摘园、垂钓中心、皮艇基地、荷园极具特色，吸引了许多艺术家来此采风、创建艺术创作基地。

其中 so... that... 意为"如此……以至于……"。that 引导一个结果状语从句，如：The birthday cake looked so delicious that the children ate it up. 那个生日蛋糕如此美味，以至于孩子们把它吃光了。so that 也引导目的状

语从句，意为"以便；为了"，相当于 in order to/so as to，常放于句中。例如：My sister made a model plane so that she could help with her friend studying the science last night. 昨天晚上我妹妹做了一个飞机模型以便她能帮助她的朋友学习科学。

Translation of the reading texts 课文译文

板辽金沙滩
——"重庆的马尔代夫"

板辽金沙滩，集生态休闲、时尚运动、激情游乐、滨湖度假四大功能于一体，是一个理想的游览胜地。长滩蜿蜒、茶山起伏、蓝天白云、绿树成荫，板辽金沙滩是目前国内最大的内陆沙滩。

板辽金沙滩位于青年镇板辽村内，湖面清幽、生态环境优越。山、湖、岛、湾、茶等相映成趣，同时其也作为重庆市水上运动基地、重庆市休闲垂钓中心、重庆市露营目的地而闻名。景区内有露营、皮艇、野炊、自助烧烤、垂钓、篝火狂欢、采茶制作、踏青登山、苗家风情演出、3D露天电影十大主题活动，其中露营基地、茶叶体验采摘园、垂钓中心、皮艇基地、荷园极具特色，吸引了许多艺术家来此采风、创建艺术创作基地，并吸引着越来越多的市内外游客来此赏景怡心、休闲度假。

风情沙滩作为板辽湖景区的热门景点，总面积 13.2 万平方米、沙滩区 9.3 万平方米。其沙滩区域地势平坦开阔，有极佳的景观视线效果。沙滩上的沙全部为海沙，从遥远的海边搬运而至，总共有 45 000 吨。风情沙滩被分为拓展活动区、休闲活动区、综合活动区三大区域，主要玩点有阳光沙滩、绿岛、无边界游泳池、水上飞人、摩托艇、荷塘蛙语等。有如此漂亮的沙滩和好玩的娱乐项目，难怪板辽金沙滩被称为"重庆的马尔代夫"。

Homework　家庭作业

After class, please make an interview to talk about Banliao Golden Beach with your partner. One is a journalist from CQTV, and the other is a local student who knows the scenic spot a lot. You are required to present your interview next class.

Lesson 13   The Mushroom Park

—A Paradise for Children

The Mushroom Park is the first mushroom-themed parent-child amusement park in China. The "giant mushrooms" hidden in the dense jungle look just like magical castles, adorned by a variety of mushroom-shaped decorations, making this park a paradise for children. The Mushroom Park consists of five areas: Parent-Child Amusement Area, Mushroom Picking Experience Area, Lotus Pond Wetland Area, Water World Area and Mushroom Theme Exploration Area. Children can search for Smurfs in the Parent-Child Amusement Area, pick mushrooms in the Mushroom Picking Experience Area, play in the Water World for fun, and adventure in the Mushroom Theme Exploration Area.

Parent-Child Amusement Area

There are lots of entertainment and experience projects for children to have fun in this area, such as Smurf Farm, Magic Forest, Mushroom Bumper Car, Giant Mushroom Swivel Flying Chair, Mushroom Theme Train and so on. Children can play hide and seek game  with Smurfs in the jungle, experience the exciting swivel flying chair, or just enjoy the beauty of the scenic spot on the mushroom theme train.

Mushroom Picking Experience Area

The Mushroom Picking Experience Area in the mushroom forest is the most popular in the Mushroom Park. There are 18 kinds of mushrooms for tourists to experience the fun of picking mushrooms by themselves, such as flammulina velutipes,  mushrooms, straw mushrooms and Lingzhi in the mushroom picking experience area. And picking mushrooms in the mushroom forest is children's favorite activity. There are also models and introductions of various kinds of mushrooms in this area,  which is helpful to enrich children's knowledge.

（本文图片由万盛发布公众号提供）

77

Words and expressions　生词和短语

adorn ［əˈdɔːn］ *vt.* 装饰；使生色

Smurf ［smɜːf］ *n.* 蓝精灵（漫画形象）

bumper car 碰碰车

swivel ［ˈswɪv(ə)l］ *vi.* 旋转

flammulina velutipes 金针菇

Lingzhi 灵芝

Notes to the texts　课文注解

1. The "giant mushrooms" hidden in the dense jungle look just like magical castles, adorned by a variety of mushroom-shaped decorations, making this park a paradise for children. 一朵朵"大蘑菇"掩映在茂密的丛林中，仿佛魔幻的城堡。各种蘑菇造型的装饰，将这里点缀成孩子们的快乐天堂。

其中 hidden in the dense jungle 为过去分词，作后置定语，修饰 mushrooms；adorned... decorations 这部分为过去分词，作状语，最后 making... for children 为现在分词，作结果状语。

2. The Mushroom Park consists of five areas: Parent-Child Amusement Area, Mushroom Picking Experience Area, Lotus Pond Wetland Area, Water World Area and Mushroom Theme Exploration Area. 蘑菇总动员主要分为五大区域：儿童亲子游乐区、菌林采菇体验区、荷塘湿地产业景观区、亲水休闲区、蘑菇主题景观探秘区。

其中 consist of 是动词短语，意为"由……组成"，相当于 be made up of。例如：The restaurant is upstairs and consists of a large, open room. 饭店在楼上，有一个宽敞的开间。

3. Children can play hide and seek game with Smurfs in the jungle, experience the exciting swivel flying chair, or just enjoy the beauty of the scenic spot on the mushroom theme train. 孩子们可以和丛林里的蓝精灵玩捉迷藏，体验令人兴奋的旋转飞椅，或者在蘑菇主题小火车上欣赏景区的美丽。

其中 hide and seek game 意为捉迷藏游戏，如：Almost all the young children like playing hide and seek game. 几乎所有的孩子都喜欢玩捉迷藏游戏。

Translation of the reading texts　课文译文

蘑菇总动员
——孩子们的天堂

蘑菇总动员是中国首个以蘑菇为主题的亲子乐园。一朵朵"大蘑菇"掩映在茂密的丛林中，仿佛魔幻的城堡。各种蘑菇造型的装饰，将这里点缀成孩子们的快乐天堂。蘑菇总动员主要分为五大区域：儿童亲子游乐区、菌林采菇体验区、荷塘湿地产业景观区、亲水休闲区、蘑菇主题景观探秘区。小伙伴们可以在儿童亲子游乐区寻找蓝精灵，可以在菌林采菇体验区采蘑菇，可以在亲水休闲区嬉戏，还可以在蘑菇主题景观探秘区冒险。

儿童亲子游乐区

儿童亲子游乐区有许多娱乐体验项目供孩子游玩，如蓝精灵农庄、魔法森林、蘑菇碰碰乐、欢乐蘑菇转转杯、大蘑菇旋转飞椅、蘑菇主题小火车等。孩子们可以和丛林里的蓝精灵玩捉迷藏，体验令人兴奋的旋转飞椅，或者在蘑菇主题小火车上欣赏景区的美丽。

菌林采菇体验区

菌林采菇体验区是蘑菇总动员最受欢迎的地方，体验区内有金针菇、香菇、草菇、灵芝等 18 种菌类，供游客体验亲手采摘蘑菇的乐趣。在菌林采摘蘑菇是每一个孩子最喜欢的活动。该区域还有关于不同种类蘑菇的模型和介绍，这有助于丰富孩子们的知识。

Homework 家庭作业

Your friend Lucy plans to visit the Mushroom Park and she writes a letter asking for some information about sights there. Please write a letter introducing it in 100 words.

Lesson 14   Sports City

-The Hometown of Badminton

There is not only a variety of food in Wansheng, but it is also a paradise for sports lovers. Therefore, you don't have to worry about the burden of food on your body in Wansheng. Perfect sports facilities and people who exercise everywhere will get you moving. Because here is the hometown of badminton, excellent athletes make great contributions to our sports atmosphere, especially the girl, Zhang Yawen.

Zhang was born in Wansheng District of Chongqing in September 1983. Her parents were mine workers. Her father gave her the name "Zhang Ya" (Later renamed as "Zhang YaWen"), which means number two in Chinese, but she became the pride of Chongqing.

Zhang started playing badminton at the age of five and entered the Chongqing Badminton Team in 1993. Once in a competition, she was injured due to overtraining. If she continued to train, the injury would probably worsen and end her sports life. But for the game, for the collective benefit, she resolutely chose to adhere to the training, with amazing perseverance against injuries. Inspired by her, the women's badminton team won the fifth place in the team, and Zhang won the fifth place in the mixed doubles.

On the night of the mixed doubles final at the Badminton World Cup in December 2005, her mother was taken seriously ill and given a warning from the

hospital. Her father hid the truth from her for fear that the news would upset her and affect the final the next day. Until Zhang finally won the first Olympic world gold medal after Chongqing became a province-level municipality, she learned of her mother's illness. In 2008, Zhang won the bronze medal in women's doubles at the Beijing Olympics, which was the first Olympic medal won by Chongqing Municipality.

Zhang Yawen pursues her dream with great efforts. She dedicates her youth and strength to create outstanding achievements, making contributions to Wansheng and Chongqing sports.

（本文图片由百度百科提供）

Words and expressions 生词和短语

paradise ['pærədaɪs] *n.* 天堂

burden ['bɜːdn] *n.* 负担

facility [fə'sɪlətɪ] *n.* 设施

badminton ['bædmɪntən] *n.* 羽毛球

overtraining [ˌəʊvə'treɪnɪŋ] *n.* 过度训练

collective [kə'lektɪv] *adj.* 集体的

resolutely ['rezəluːtlɪ] *adv.* 坚决地

adhere [əd'hɪə(r)] *v.* 遵循

mixed doubles 混合双打

municipality [mjuːˌnɪsɪ'pælətɪ] *n.* 自治市

Notes to the texts   课文注解

1. There is not only a variety of food in Wansheng, but it is also a paradise for sports lovers. 万盛不仅有各种各样的美食，还是运动爱好者的天堂。

Not only... but also...，意为"不仅……而且……"。例如：She's not only a great dramatic actress but she's also very humorous. 她不仅是一位优秀的女戏剧演员，而且也很幽默。

2. Perfect sports facilities and people who exercise everywhere will get you moving. 完善的运动设施、随处可见的运动的人，让你也不知不觉动起来。

"who exercise everywhere" 为定语从句，修饰前面的先行词 people，关系代词 who 在从句中充当主语。例如：A new master will come tomorrow who will teach you German. 明天要来一位新教师教你们德语。

3. Zhang was born in Wansheng District of Chongqing in September 1983. 张（亚雯）1983 年 9 月出生于重庆市万盛区。

be born in 在文中意为"出生于"。例如：I was born in Toronto. 我出生于多伦多。

Translation of the reading texts   课文译文

运动之城
——羽毛球之乡

万盛不仅有各种各样的美食，还是运动爱好者的天堂。所以到万盛，你不用担心美食带给你的身体负担。完善的运动设施、随处可见的运动的人，让你也不知不觉动起来。这里是羽毛球之乡，优秀的运动健儿们为我们城市的运动氛围营造作出了巨大的贡献，尤其是张亚雯这个女孩。

张亚雯，1983 年 9 月出生于重庆市万盛区。她的父母都是矿区工作人员。父亲没有按字辈来取名，给她取了个名字"张亚"（后来改名为"张亚雯"），中文"亚"字表示的是第二名，可她后来却成了重庆市的骄傲。

张亚雯5岁开始练习羽毛球，1993年正式进入重庆市羽毛球队。在一次比赛前，她因训练过度受伤，若继续训练，伤情极有可能恶化，断送运动生命。但为了比赛，为了集体的利益，她毅然选择了坚持训练，以惊人的毅力对抗伤病。在她的带领下，最终羽毛球女队夺得团体第五名的好成绩，张亚雯个人夺得混合双打第五名。

在2005年12月结束的世界杯羽毛球赛中，张亚雯混合双打进入决赛的当晚，她母亲突然病情加重住进医院，医生已下达了病危通知书。父亲怕这一消息扰乱她的情绪，影响第二天的决赛，便对她隐瞒了实情。直到张亚雯终于夺得重庆直辖后第一个奥运项目世界冠军，她才得知母亲的病情。2008年，张亚雯在北京奥运会上获得羽毛球女双铜牌，这是重庆直辖后获得的第一块奥运奖牌。

张亚雯以不懈的努力追逐着自己的梦想。她奉献青春和力量，创造出优异的成绩，为万盛和重庆的体育事业添砖加瓦！

Summary writing 摘要写作

Answer the questions and briefly introduce Zhang Yawen within 50 words.

1. Where does Zhang come from?

2. What is the meaning of her name in Chinese?

3. What spirits can we see from her?

Homework 家庭作业

Your friend Lucy wants to know more famous people in Wansheng. Can you find more information on the Internet or books to send to her?

UNIT 3 Profound Cultural Heritage
文化底蕴

Lesson 15　Colourful Folkways

Folkway not only enriches people's life, but also increases national cohesion. The author lists two important folk festivals in Wansheng.

Jumping Flower Festival

"Jumping Flower Festival" is a traditional folkway of Miao people in Wansheng, which is mainly to celebrate the harvest, court and visit friends or relatives. The main activities are  bullfighting, shooting bulls, praying to the gods, climbing flower poles, drinking horn wine, climbing a mountain of swords, plunging into the sea of flames, singing, dancing, etc.

Since Wansheng successfully held the first "Jumping Flower Festival" in 1998, this annual festival is always on a grand scale, attracting groups of tourists from all over the world. The current "Jumping Flower Festival" has main-  tained the original characteristics, showing Miao people's work, life, sacrifice, marriage and funeral folk customs. In addition, Miao costumes and handicrafts are more than delicate and exquisite, astonishing to the eyes.

Tea Plucking Festival

Tea Plucking Festival is a grand gathering for the tea industry and a stage to carry forward Wansheng tea culture and show the charm of tea. At the same time, it is also the best rural tour for tourists to drink tea, enjoy leisure, get close to nature and feel the beauty of ecology and harmony.

Every March, Wansheng District Cultural Tourism Office will hold a Tea Plucking Festival at the Dicuijianming Tea Garden in the Black Valley attraction. Visitors can put on delicate Miao costumes and pluck tea using bamboo baskets on their backs with folk songs from the tea hills. At the scene, fried tea demonstration and tea ceremony performances and other activities will be held. Visitors are also free to visit scenic spots such as Black Valley and Miao Village to experience the pleasures of rural leisure tourism and red tourism.

Holding folk culture activities can not only deepen people's understanding of the traditional culture but also promote the inheritance and development of folk culture.

（本文图片由万盛发布公众号提供）

Words and expressions　生词和短语

folkway ['fəuk,weɪ] *n.* 民俗

festival ['festɪvl] *n.* 节日

celebrate ['selɪbreɪt] *vt.* 祝贺

court [kɔːt] *vt.* 求爱；企图获得

pray [preɪ] *vi.* 祈祷

plunge [plʌndʒ] *vt.* 猛冲向；暴跌；骤降

annual [ˈænjʊəl] *adj.* 年度的

attract [əˈtrækt] *vt.* 吸引

scale [skeil] *n.* 规模

maintain [meɪnˈteɪn] *vt.* 维修

custom [ˈkʌstəm] *n.* 风俗

exquisite [ɪkˈskwɪzɪt] *adj.* 精美的

delicate [ˈdelɪkɪt] *adj.* 精美的

pluck [plʌk] *vt.* 采，摘

rural [ˈrʊərəl] *adj.* 农村的

demonstration [ˌdemənsˈtreɪʃən] *n.* 演示

Notes to the texts　课文注解

1. "Jumping Flower Festival" is a traditional folkway of Miao people in Wansheng, which is mainly to celebrate the harvest, court and visit friends or relatives. 踩山会是万盛区苗族同胞的一项传统民俗文化集会，主要是欢庆丰收、谈情说爱、会亲访友。

which 引导一个非限制性定语从句。定语从句有限制性和非限制性两种。限制性定语从句是句中不可缺少的部分，去掉它主句意思往往不明确；非限制性定语从句是对先行词的附加说明，去掉了也不会影响主句的意思，它与主句之间通常用逗号分开，将非限制性定语从句放在句子中间，其前后都需要用逗号隔开。

2. Since Wansheng successfully held the first "Jumping Flower Festival" in 1998, this annual festival is always on a grand scale, attracting groups of tourists from all over the world. 万盛自 1998 年成功举办首届万盛苗族踩山会以来，一年一届，届届规模盛大，吸引着一批又一批海内外游客前来观光。

attracting 是非谓语中的现在分词，作结果状语。作状语是非谓语动词

的主要功能之一。例如：He got up late, being late for school。他起床晚了，导致他上学迟到了。

3. In addition, Miao costumes and handicrafts are more than delicate and exquisite, astonishing to the eyes. 此外，苗族服饰和工艺品也让人目不暇接。

more than 意为"不仅仅是；不止；非常；超过"。not more than 为否定式。no more than 意为"仅仅；只有，强调少"。例如：He is more than a father。他不仅仅是一名父亲。又如：I have not more than 5 books. 我只有 5 本书。再如：She is no more than an ordinary girl. 她只不过是一个普通女孩。

4. Holding folk culture activities can not only deepen people's understanding of the traditional literature, but also promote the inheritance and development of folk culture. 举办民俗文化活动，不仅可以加深人们对传统文化的理解，还可以推动民俗文化的传承和发展。

Holding 是动名词，作主语。例如：Reading is my favorite. 阅读是我的最爱。not only... but also 是英语中比较常见的一个关联词组，用于连接两个表示并列关系的成分，着重强调后者，它的意思是"不但……而且……"，其中的 also 有时可以省略。例如：Not only I but also he likes English. 不但我喜欢英语，他也喜欢英语。

Translation of the reading texts 课文译文

多彩民俗

民俗文化既丰富了人们的生活，又增加了民族凝聚力。笔者列举了万盛两个具有重要意义的民俗节日。

踩山会

踩山会是万盛区苗族同胞的一项传统民俗文化集会，主要是欢庆丰收、谈情说爱、会亲访友。踩山会主要有对歌、射箭、斗牛、打牛、祭神还愿、爬花杆、喝牛角酒、上刀山下火海、吹芦笙、跳唱、赛歌、赛舞等。

万盛自 1998 年成功举办首届万盛苗族踩山会以来，一年一届，届届规模盛大，吸引着一批又一批海内外游客前来观光。现在的踩山会保持了原来的特色，表现了苗族同胞劳动、生活、祭祀、婚丧等民风民俗。此外，苗族服饰和工艺品也让人目不暇接。

采茶节

采茶节是茶界的一次盛会，是弘扬万盛茶文化、展现茶魅力的舞台，同时也让广大游客品茗休闲、亲近自然，感受生态之美、和谐之美。

每年的 3 月，万盛区文旅办都会在黑山谷景区的滴翠剑名茶园举行采茶节。游客可以换上精美的苗族服装、背上竹编的背篓采茶。其间伴随着从茶山传来的阵阵山歌。采茶节现场将举行炒茶演示和茶道表演等活动。游客还可以自由参观黑山谷和苗寨等景点，体验农村休闲旅游和红色旅游的乐趣。

举办民俗文化活动，不仅可以加深人们对传统文化的理解，还可以推动民俗文化的传承和发展。

Summary writing　摘要写作

Your friend Jack plans to learn about folkways of Wansheng and he writes a letter asking for some information about it. Please write a letter introducing one or two festivals within 100 words.

Homework 家庭作业

Answer the questions and briefly introduce one of Wansheng's festivals using less than 50 words.

1. When was the first Jumping Flower Festival held?

2. What are the main activities of Jumping Flower Festival?

3. When and where does Tea Plucking Festival take place?

4. What are the activity arrangements of the Tea Plucking Festival?

5. Why are these activities meaningful?

Lesson 16   The Most Beautiful
Miao Costume

There is a branch of Miao ethnic minority Red Miao in Wansheng. Its rich and colorful culture is the treasure of Chinese culture. Miao costume is an important embodiment of Miao culture. Miao costume style is various. There are more than 200 styles. Miao costume is the most significant costume among all ethnic costumes in China, which is not only a wonderful work in Chinese culture but also a treasure of historical culture. This paragraph will introduce the Miao costume from the Miao handmade embroidery, costume patterns and headdresses.

Handmade Embroidery

The Miao handmade embroidery is one of the leading components of the Miao costume, representing the highest embroider techniques of the Chinese minorities. The main artistic features of handmade embroidery are the neat and clean pattern, fresh and elegant colors and diversified stit-

ches. It is more than delicate, which boasts the best workmanship, strong elements of local folk culture and the characteristics of Miao ethnic minority.

Their embroidered animals, flowers and birds are lifelike. The pattern usually features butterflies flying in blooming flowers and grasses. It is believed that butterflies will bring happiness and when flowers are in full blossom, good fortune will arrive.

Patterns of Miao Costume

Legend has it that the ancestors of the Miao people, the Chi You Tribe, migrated from the Yellow River to the Yangtze River. Because there was no written record, the emperor asked women to embroider their national history into their clothes for the preservation of national memory. The two yellow-green lines on the clothes represent the Yellow River and the Yangtze River. The three red, blue and green lines symbolize their migration routes. Therefore, the Miao costume pattern has the function of remembering ancestors and inheriting history.

Red Headdress

The indispensable nature of headdress in the costumes of Miao ethnic minority is fully explained in the style how Miao people dress themselves in Wansheng. Their headdress is extremely delicate. Ladies usually wear their hair in a high coil decorated by jewelries together with earrings, pendants and ear-pillars.

（本文图片由万盛发布公众号提供）

94

Words and expressions   生词和短语

ethnic ［ˈeθnɪk］ *adj.* 民族的

minority ［maɪˈnɒrətɪ］ *n.* 少数民族

treasure ［ˈtreʒə］ *n.* 珠宝，珍宝

costume ［ˈkɒstjuːm］ *n.* 服装

various ［ˈveərɪəs］ *adj.* 各种各样的

magnificent ［mægˈnɪfɪs(ə)nt］ *a.* 杰出的

embroidery ［ɪmˈbrɔɪdərɪ］ *n.* 绣花

component ［kəmˈpəʊnənt］ *n.* 成分

stitch ［stɪtʃ］ *n.* 针脚

boast ［bəʊst］ *vi.* 夸耀

characteristic ［ˌkærəktəˈrɪstɪk］ *n.* 特征

blooming ［ˈbluːmɪŋ］ *a.* 开花；兴旺

fortune ［ˈfɔːtʃuːn］ *n.* 运气；财富

migrate ［maɪˈɡreɪt］ *vi.* 移居

preservation ［ˌprezəˈveɪʃn］ *n.* 维护

represent ［ˌreprɪˈzent］ *vt.* 代表；象征

inherit ［ɪnˈherɪt］ *v.* 继承

indispensable ［ˌɪndɪsˈpensəbl］ *a.* 不可缺少

headdress ［ˈheddres］ *n.* 首饰；头饰

decorate ［ˈdekəˌreɪt］ *vt.* 装饰

Notes to the texts　课文注解

1. Miao costume is an important embodiment of Miao culture. 苗族服饰是苗族文化的重要体现。

embodiment 意为"体现、具象"。可依据文章上下文的含义来推测，训练猜词能力。

2. The Miao handmade embroidery is one of the leading ornaments of the Miao costume, representing the highest embroider techniques of the Chinese minorities. 苗族刺绣是苗族服饰中最主要的装饰之一，代表着我国少数民族刺绣的最高技艺。

representing 系非谓语，作状语。例如：They went to the park, singing and dancing. 他们边唱边说向公园走去。the highest 是最高级用法。例如：He is the tallest boy in the class. 他是班上最高的男孩。

3. It is more than delicate, boasting the best workmanship, strong elements of local folk culture and the characteristics of Miao ethnic minority. 绣工精巧细腻绝伦，富有浓郁的民间、民族特色。

more than 修饰数词，表示超过的含义；修饰形容词表示非常的含义。boasting 引导非谓语短语，作伴随状语。

4. It is believed that butterflies will bring happiness and when flowers are in full blossom, good fortune will arrive. 人们认为蝴蝶寓意福气满满，花开富贵同时也表达了好运连连。

It 是形式主语，that 引导的句子为真正的主语从句，主语从句中嵌套一个时间状语从句。例如：It is unbelievable that he has been admitted by Peking University. 真不可思议，他考上了北京大学。

5. Legend has it that the ancestors of the Miao people, the Chi You Tribe, migrated from the Yellow River to the Yangtze River. 传说苗族祖先蚩尤部落

在黄河和长江之间不断迁徙。

Legend has it that... 意为"传说……"。Yellow River 黄河, Yangtze River 长江。

Translation of the reading texts   课文译文

最美苗族服饰

在万盛有一支苗族的分支红头苗。它丰富多彩的苗族文化，是中华文化的瑰宝。苗族服饰是苗族文化的重要体现。苗族服饰样式繁多，有200多种。苗族服饰是我国所有民族服饰中最为华丽的服饰，既是中华文化中的一朵奇葩，也是历史文化的瑰宝。本文将从苗族手工刺绣、服饰图案和头饰三方面来介绍苗族服饰。

手工刺绣

苗族刺绣是苗族服饰中最主要的装饰之一，代表着我国少数民族刺绣的最高技艺。手工刺绣的主要艺术特点是图案工整娟秀，色彩清新高雅，针法丰富，雅艳相宜，绣工精巧细腻绝伦，富有浓郁的民间、民族特色。作品图案中有花有草，还有飞舞的蝴蝶，其中蝴蝶寓意福气满满，花开富贵，同时也表达了好运连连。

苗族服装图案

传说，苗族祖先蚩尤部落在黄河和长江之间不断迁徙。由于当时没有文字记载，为保存民族记忆，先祖令女人将民族的历史缝刺在衣服上。苗族服饰纵横交错的图案代表田园，两条黄绿色线条分别代表黄河、长江，三条红、蓝、绿线条代表迁徙路线。因此苗族服饰上面的图案具有怀念先祖和传承历史的作用。

红苗头饰

苗族头饰是苗族服饰不可缺少的一部分，展示了苗族妇女的穿搭风格。她们的头饰非常精致。万盛的红头苗头饰华丽精巧。妇女一般挽高髻于顶，以珠宝来装饰，辅以耳环、耳坠、耳柱等饰物。

Summary writing 摘要写作

Your friend Lucy plans to learn about Miao costume and she writes a letter asking for some information about it. Please write a letter introducing one or two elements of Miao costume in 100 words.

Homework 家庭作业

Answer the questions and briefly introduce one element of Miao costume using less than 50 words.

1. Which branch of Miao people live in Wansheng?

2. What are the main artistic features of handmade embroidery?

3. What does the pattern butterflies and flowers mean?

4. What decorations are on the red headdress?

Lesson 17　Spiritual Culture

Wansheng spirit takes the feelings of loving the motherland and homeland as the main content, shaping Wansheng's urban temperament and cultural connotation from the perspective of history and reality.

The Spirit of Dedication

Numerous talents have achieved great merits and achievements, established outstanding moral integrity that benefit the neighbors, and are renowned far away. Luo Chuntang developed hot spring, Deng Jiuxian donated to build bridges, Chen Zedong set up

schools, Seng Zongyi helped the poor people in trouble, You Hailong participated in "Gongche Shangshu Movement", and these countryside celebrities showed us dedication spirit and great love.

The Spirit of Red Revolutionary

During the War of Resistance Against Japanese Aggression, Wansheng poured out a large number of patriots and sent a large number of fighter planes to the battlefield. Liu Ziru, 67 years old, organized a Chongqing field service

regiment and served the soldiers in the front line for three years. Chen Zhijun, Wang Shiming, Zhu Kai, Mei Huaiqing and other patriots left immortal memories to Wansheng with their fearless revolutionary spirit. The military based in Haikongdong successively produced nearly 100 fighter planes, which made great historical contributions to the victory of the War of Resistance Against Japanese Aggression. Wansheng people will always tell red stories and inherit red genes.

The Spirit of Filial Piety

The legend had it that there was a dutiful son, living together with his old mother and taking care of her carefully. While wading across a dangerous river to deliver food to his mother, he was carried away by the flood. People sighed that he must die, but he survived after being swept away by the waves for miles. The villagers believed that the dutiful son moved the god, so they renamed the river Xiaozi River. For thousands of years, Xiaozi River has nurtured a strong spirit of filial piety. In recent years, Wansheng has emerged a large number of filial models, such as, Yang Nengxian, the "national star of 100 filial piety".

Wansheng has profound humanistic atmosphere and cultural heritage, which will always be spread and inherited.

（本文图片由万盛博物馆提供）

Words and expressions   生词和短语

spirit［ˈspɪrɪt］*n.* 精神；灵魂

connotation［ˌkɒnəˈteɪʃ(ə)n］*n.* 含义

temperament［ˈtemprəmənt］*n.* 性情

perspective［pəˈspektɪv］*n.* 观点

talent［ˈtælənt］*n.* 人才

establish［ɪˈstæblɪʃ］*vt.* 建立

moral［ˈmɒrl］*adj.* 道德上的

participate［pɑːˈtɪsɪˌpeɪt］*vi.* 参加

patriot［ˈpeɪtrɪət］*n.* 爱国者

immortal［ɪˈmɔːt(ə)l］*adj.* 永生的

integrity［ɪnˈtegrətɪ］*n.* 正直，诚实

revolutionary［ˌrevəˈluːʃənərɪ］*a.* 革命的

contribution［ˌkɒntrɪˈbjuːʃ(ə)n］*n.* 贡献

filial piety 孝顺

wade［weɪd］*vi.* 涉；蹚

nurture［ˈnɜːrtʃər］*v.* 培育，教养

atmosphere［ˈætməsfɪə(r)］*n.* 氛围

inherit［ɪnˈherɪt］*vt.* 继承

Notes to the texts   课文注解

1. Wansheng spirit takes the feelings of loving the motherland and homeland as the main content, shaping Wansheng's urban temperament and cultural connotation from the perspective of history and reality. 万盛精神以爱祖国、爱家乡的

家国情怀为主线，从历史和现实的角度塑造了万盛的城市气质和人文内蕴。

take... as 意思是"把……看作是"。例如：They are friendly with her and take her as their best friend. 他们对她很友好并把她看作是最好的朋友。shaping 为非谓语，作结果状语。

2. Numerous talents have achieved great merits and achievements and established outstanding moral integrity that benefit the neighbors, and are renowned far away. 无数仁人志士建功立德，恩泽乡邻，蜚声远方。

that benefit... 为定语从句，修饰先行词 achievements and integrity。例如：He is the person that I am looking for. 他就是我正在寻找的人。

3. The military based in Haikongdong successively produced nearly 100 fighter planes, which made great historical contributions to the victory of the War of Resistance Against Japanese Aggression. 海孔洞的军工基地陆续生产了近百架战斗机，为抗战胜利作出了巨大历史贡献。

based in 为非谓语中的过去分词短语，作后置定语。例如：The boy praised by the teacher is a good boy. 被老师表扬的那个孩子是个好孩子。which 引导非限制性定语从句。例如：He was a little nervous in front of so many people, which is understandable. 在如此众多人面前他有点紧张，这是可以理解的。

4. The legend had it that there was a dutiful son, living together with his old mother and taking care of her carefully. 相传，万盛出了一个孝子，与老母相依为命。

The legend had it that... 为固定搭配，表示传闻的意思，that 后面跟从句。living 和 taking 是非谓语短语，作伴随状语。

5. While wading across a dangerous river to deliver food to his mother, he was carried away by the flood. 在涉险过河为母亲送饭时，他被洪水卷走。

While wading 为省略句型。当主从句主语一致，且从句的谓语中含有 be 动词时，省略从句中的主语和 be 动词。

Translation of the reading texts   课文译文

精神文化

万盛精神以爱祖国、爱家乡的家国情怀为主线，从历史和现实的角度塑造了万盛的城市气质和人文内蕴。

奉献精神

无数仁人志士建功立德，恩泽乡邻，蜚声远方。罗春堂开发温汤、邓九先捐资筑桥、陈泽东设馆教学、僧宗益解困济危、犹海龙"公车上书"，一个个乡贤先烈谱写着奉献精神和大爱情怀。

革命精神

在抗战时期，万盛涌现出大批爱国志士，并为战场输送了大量战机。爱国志士刘子如实干兴邦、慈善济困、精忠报国，堪为时代楷模。在抗战期间，年已 67 岁的刘子如，组织了一个 70 多人的重庆战地服务团，为将士服务，在前线整整工作了 3 年。陈治均、汪石冥、朱凯、梅怀清等志士不怕牺牲的革命精神，也留给万盛不朽的记忆。海孔洞的军工基地陆续生产了近百架战斗机，为抗战的胜利作出了巨大的历史贡献。万盛人会一直讲述红色故事，并传承红色基因。

孝慈精神

相传，万盛出了一个孝子，他与老母亲相依为命。在涉险过河为母亲送饭时，他被洪水卷走。人们叹息这位孝子必死无疑，谁料他被浪卷去数里后，竟得以生还。乡人认为是这位孝子的孝行感动了上天，于是，将河流改名为"孝子河"。千百年来，孝子河孕育了浓厚的孝慈精神。近年，万盛涌现了一大批孝老爱亲的典型，如 30 年如一日照顾孤老的"全国百名孝亲敬老之星"杨能仙。

万盛有深厚的文化底蕴和人文气息。万盛人文将一直绵延。

Summary writing　摘要写作

Your friend Li Hua plans to learn about Wansheng humanities culture and she writes a letter asking for some information about it. Please write a letter introducing it in 100 words.

Homework　家庭作业

Answer the questions and briefly introduce Wansheng humanities culture using less than 50 words.

1. Which celebrities are mentioned in Paragraph 1?

2. What contribution did Liu Zilu make to the War of Resistance Against Japanese Aggression?

3. Why is the river called the Xiaozi River?

Lesson 18   Pleasant Music

Music is the language of human communication and traditional music, which is passed on from generation to generation, is the treasure of all of us. The unique geographical environment and human history of Wansheng has created a large amount of traditional music with regional characteristics. Many kinds of music are still commonly used in people's daily life.

The Reed-Pipe Wind Instrument

Miao people are good at singing and dancing. They always sing and dance during wedding and funeral events, festivals, visiting and courting, which have been handed down from generation to generation in the long history. Every family of Miao ethnic minority has a reed-pipe wind instrument and almost all of them can dance. People usually dance to the songs played by the reed-pipe wind instrument or drum. The rhythm of the music is bright and cheerful, and the mood is high. It shows the plain, unrestrained national character, hardworking and kindhearted spirit of the Miao people in Wansheng.

The reed-pipe wind instrument music of the Miao ethnic minority has many musical representative works, such as "Stepping on the Hall Song" "Entering the

Hall Song" and "Match Song". The original song of "Happy Miao Mountain" in Wansheng District is created according to the folk tunes of red Miao. The melody is lively and warm, while the lyrics are simple, fresh and beautiful, reflecting the unique Miao culture.

Ensemble of Wind and Percussion Instruments of Jinqiao

Ensemble of Wind and Percussion Instruments of Jinqiao is the folk music of Jinqiao Town, Wansheng District. Its musical types include festival, production, life, funeral types and so on. It has the characteristics of wide range, large volume, thick intensity, bright timbre, strong penetrating power, etc. Various music chapters are full of unique local characteristics and artistic styles. It's the essence of the ensemble of wind and percussion instruments of Bashu and was included as the national intangible cultural heritage in 2006.

The songs of ensemble of Wind and Percussion Instruments of Jinqiao reached more than one thousand. The original song "Chatting Happy Life" shows a new era rural prosperity and happy life scene, and express es the people's pursuit of a better life.

Among the numerous intangible cultural heritage of Wansheng, this traditional music is undoubtedly one of the shining pearls.

（本文图片由万盛发布公众号提供）

Words and expressions　生词和短语

generation [ˌdʒenəˈreɪʃn] *n.* 一代（人）

geographical [ˌdʒiːəˈɡræfɪk(ə)l] *adj.* 地理的

regional [ˈriːdʒənl] *adj.* 地区的

instrument [ˈɪnstrəmənt] *n.* 乐器

unrestrained [ˈʌnrɪˈstreɪnd] *a.* 无拘束的

representative [ˌreprɪˈzentətɪv] *n.* 代表

various [ˈveərɪəs] *a.* 各种各样的

unique [juˈniːk] *a.* 唯一的

artistic [ɑːˈtɪstɪk] *a.* 艺术家的

pursuit [pəˈsjuːt] *n.* 追求，追逐

intensity [ɪnˈtensətɪ] *n.* 强度

district [ˈdɪstrɪkt] *n.* 地区

essence [ˈes(ə)ns] *n.* 本质

prosperity [prɒˈsperətɪ] *n.* 兴旺

undoubtedly [ʌnˈdaʊtɪdlɪ] *adv.* 确实地

pearl [pɜːl] *n.* 珍珠

Notes to the texts　课文注解

1. Music is the language of human communication and traditional music, which is passed on from generation to generation, is the treasure of all of us. 音乐是人类交流的语言，而经过世代传承的传统音乐，则是我们全人类的财富。

which is passed on 系非限制性定语从句。

2. They always sing and dance during wedding and funeral events, festivals, visiting and courting, which have been handed down from generation to generation in the long history. 苗族在婚丧庆典、逢年过节、走亲访友、谈情说爱时，均不离歌与舞，并在悠久历史中代代相传。

which 引导非限制性定语从句。have been handed down 运用的时态是现在完成时。

3. Among the numerous intangible cultural heritage of Wansheng, this traditional music is undoubtedly one of the shining pearls. 在万盛众多的非物质文化遗产中，这些传统音乐无疑是其中一颗耀眼的明珠。

intangible cultural heritage 意为 "非物质文化遗产"。此句运用比喻的修辞手法，将金桥吹打这种传统音乐比作发光的珍珠，是对其的一种赞扬。

Translation of the reading texts　课文译文

愉悦音韵

音乐是人类交流的语言，而经过世代传承的传统音乐，则是我们全人类的财富。万盛独特的地理环境和人文历史，造就了一大批极富地域特色的传统音乐，许多音乐到现在都活跃在人们的日常生活中。

芦笙舞乐

苗族能歌善舞，在婚丧庆典、逢年过节、走亲访友、谈情说爱时，均不离歌与舞，并在悠久历史中代代相传。万盛苗族家家有歌舞芦笙，几乎个个会跳舞，舞蹈由芦笙或击鼓相伴。音乐节奏欢快明朗，情绪饱满高昂，表现出万盛区苗族人民朴素粗犷豪放的民族性格和勤劳勇敢善良的精神风貌。

苗族芦笙乐曲有众多悦耳的代表作：《踩堂曲》《进堂曲》和《比赛

曲》等。万盛原创歌曲《幸福苗山》运用红苗芦笙舞民间曲调创作而成，旋律悠扬、轻快热烈，歌词简洁清新优美，歌唱出独特的苗家文化。

金桥吹打

金桥吹打是万盛区金桥镇的民间音乐，属于吹打乐种，有喜庆类、生产生活类、丧事类等类别。金桥吹打有音域宽、音量大、力度厚、音色明快、穿透力强等特点。金桥吹打曲目繁多，具有鲜明的地方特色和艺术风格，是巴渝吹打的精华部分，在 2006 年入选中国国家级非物质文化遗产。

金桥吹打的曲目有一千余首。万盛原创歌曲《龙门阵·幸福生活》通过金桥唢呐与传统打击乐欢快热烈的情景演绎，展现出新时代农村一片欣欣向荣的幸福生活场景，同时也表达了万盛儿女对美好生活的热爱。

在万盛众多的非物质文化遗产中，这些传统音乐无疑是其中一颗耀眼的明珠。

Summary writing　摘要写作

Your friend Lily plans to learn about instruments and she writes a letter asking for some information about them. Please write a letter introducing instruments in 100 words.

Homework　家庭作业

Answer the questions and briefly introduce the reed-pipe wind instrument or the Ensemble of Wind and Percussion Instruments of Jinqiao（金桥吹打）*using less than 50 words.*

1. What are the representative songs of the reed-pipe wind instrument?

2. What is the musical style of songs of the reed-pipe wind instrument?

3. How many types can the songs of the Ensemble of Wind and Percussion Instruments of Jinqiao fall into?

4. What is the musical style of songs of the Ensemble of Wind and Percussion Instruments of Jinqiao?

UNIT 4   Delicious Food
特色美食

Lesson 19   Various Liquors in Wansheng

If you are a real lover of liquor, Wansheng is a good place to visit. There are various liquors which can meet your taste.

Liquor Made of Kiwi Fruits

Liquor made of wild kiwi fruits in Jiuguoqing dates back to 2005 and has passed ISO 9001:2000 certification. If it is taken in an adequate amount for a long-term, your physical health will be strengthened as muscles and bones are relaxed and blood veins unclogged.

Liquor Made of Roxburgh Rose

This specialty was developed in 2005 by soaking wild Roxburgh rose in strong liquor which is brewed out of 100% grains. Usually, it is stored in cellar for three years and no edible alcohol is added.

Liquor of Black Valley

The brewers choose only the clear spring and brook water from the valley. People living in Hongcaofang take stream water in Black Valley to produce liquor with ancient techniques lasting for thousands of years. When it is retrieved from the storage of constant temperature and moisture, it smells intoxicating and tastes very soft.

The Sucked Home Brew

The sucked home brew, a traditional and unique beverage for the people of Miao ethnic minority, is also known as the home brew of bamboo tube or of bamboo pipe because it is supposed to be sucked up by a narrow and long bamboo tube. Some experts believe that it is the prototype of Wuliangye, a famous Chinese liquor.

（本文图片由重庆红苗文化旅游发展股份有限公司提供）

Words and expressions　生词和短语

liquor［'lɪkər］*n.* 酒，含酒精饮料

certification［ˌsɜːtɪfɪ'keɪʃn］*n.* 证明，鉴定

adequate［'ædɪkwət］*adj.* 充足的；适当的

strengthen［'streŋθn］*vt.* 加强；巩固

beverage［'bevərɪdʒ］*n.* 饮料

vein［veɪn］*n.* 血管

unclog［ʌn'klɒg］*vt.* 使畅通

soak［'səʊk］*v.* 浸泡；使湿透

brew［bruː］*v.* 酿造

cellar［'selər］*n.* 地窖

edible［'edəb(ə)l］*adj.* 可食用的

brook［brʊk］*n.* 小溪，小河

moisture［'mɔɪstʃə(r)］*n.* 水分；湿度

intoxicating［ɪn'tɒksɪkeɪtɪŋ］*adj.* 令人陶醉的

suck［sʌk］*vt.* 吸吮

tube［tju:b］*n.* 管

prototype［'prəutətaɪp］*n.* 原型；最初形态

kiwi fruit 猕猴桃

Notes to the texts　课文注解

1. Liquor made of wild kiwi fruits in Jiuguoqing dates back to 2005 and has passed ISO 9001:2000 certification. 九锅箐猕猴桃酒研制于 2005 年，采用九锅箐野生原生态猕猴桃，通过 ISO 9001:2000 国际质量体系认证。

date back to 此处短语意为"追溯到"。例如：This tradition can date back to the Tang Dynasty. 这一传统可以追溯到唐朝。

2. Because it is supposed to be sucked up by a narrow and long bamboo tube. 因其用竹管咂饮而得名。

be supposed to 在文中意为"应该做某事"。例如：The hill is supposed to be the resting place of the legendary King Lud. 据说，这座山是传说中的路德国王休息的地方。

be sucked up 在文中意为"被……吸上来"。例如：The wet weight can be sucked up into the wind drying tube. 湿重颗粒能被风吸起进入干燥管。

Translation of the reading texts　课文译文

多滋多味的万盛酒

如果你是一个饮酒爱好者，万盛是一个好去处，多滋多味的万盛酒可以满足你的口味。

猕猴桃酒

九锅箐猕猴桃酒研制于 2005 年，采用九锅箐野生原生态猕猴桃，通过 ISO 9001:2000 国际质量体系认证。人们长期适量饮用，能舒筋活络，增强体质，有益健康。

刺梨酒

九锅箐刺梨酒研制于 2005 年，其泡制原料全部采用原生态野生刺梨，白酒选用纯粮食酒，窖藏三年，不含食用酒精。

黑山谷酒

采山涧珍贵清泉，匠心酿酒的初心上选，红槽坊人甄选黑山谷生态山泉水，精研几千年古法酿酒工艺，天然恒温，恒湿窖藏，酒体丰满，酒香浓郁，口感绵柔。

咂酒

咂酒，古称"筒酒""竿儿酒"等，因其用竹管咂饮而得名。它是苗族人民特有的一种传统饮料。有些学者认为咂酒可以看作中国名酒五粮液最早的雏形。

Summary writing 摘要写作

Answer the questions and give a brief introduction of various liquors in Wansheng within 60 words.

1. How many kinds of liquors are introduced in the text?

2. What makes the Sucked Home Brew famous?

3. What advantages do Liquor Made of Kiwi Fruits have?

Homework 家庭作业

Your friend Tom is interested in various liquors in Wansheng, and he wrote a letter for some information about it. Please write a letter to introduce it to him within 100 words.

Lesson 20　A Bite of Black Valley

Black Valley is famous for its unique natural scenery. However, the food here is also one of the attractions.

Heishan Black Tea

The mountains stretching along the lake shore are the place in Wansheng, where the famous "Dicuijianming" tea in Chongqing is produced. Each year, the hospitable locals will play host to numerous visitors and friends old or new, serving them with the newly produced tea.

This is a kind of black tea categorized as Heishan Black Tea (Tea of Black Valley) and it must be collected from high mountains and deep valleys before the solar term of Pure Brightness. Only the nascent buds could be picked as required. It is well shaped and in the color of moisturized pitch-black; the boiled leaf soup shows bright orange and smells charmingly fragrant.

Quadrate Bamboo Shoots of Black Valley

Known as the King in Bamboo Shoots, the quadrate bamboo shoots stand out in nature and are unique in China. The thick shoots taste tender and deliciously fresh. Since they grow up in unpolluted mountains, only the most delicacy title matches its quality.

Kiwi Fruits of Black Valley

It is in the natural mountainous environment at an altitude of 700 to 1 000 meters that high-quality and healthy kiwi fruits of Black Valley are cultivated. No pesticides or chemical fertilizers are used. One bite, life-long memory.

Bacon of Black Valley

Bacon of Black Valley is made of selected quality pork strictly in line with ISO 9001:2008. As its salty taste is moderate and in traditional style, it is the best present to friends and the primary choice to receive guests.

Delicious food in Black Valley is too numerous to mention. Do you want to have a taste?

（本文图片由重庆红苗文化旅游发展股份有限公司提供）

Words and expressions   生词和短语

stretch ［stretʃ］ *v.* 伸展，延续

hospitable ［hɒˈspɪtəb(ə)l］ *adj.* 热情友好的

categorize ［ˈkætəgəraɪz］ *v.* 分类

nascent ［ˈneɪs(ə)nt］ *adj.* 新生的

bud ［bʌd］ *n.* 嫩芽

moisturize ［ˈmɔɪstʃəraɪz］ *v.* 变潮湿

fragrant ［ˈfreɪgrənt］ *adj.* 芳香的

quadrate ［kwɒdrɪt］ *n.* 正方形的

altitude ［ˈæltɪtjuːd］ *n.* 高度；海拔

fertilizer ［ˈfɜːtəlaɪzə(r)］ *n.* 肥料

moderate ［ˈmɒdərət］ *adj.* 温和的

fragrance ［ˈfreɪgrəns］ *n.* 芳香

cultivate ［ˈkʌltɪveɪt］ *vt.* 培养

tender ［ˈtendɔ(r)］ *adj.* 柔软的

Notes to the texts   课文注解

1. The mountains stretching along the lake shore are the place in Wansheng, where the famous "Dicuijianming" tea in Chongqing is produced. 湖岸上连绵的茶山，是重庆名茶"滴翠剑名"的产地。

此句为主从复合句，其中关系副词 where 引导非限制性定语从句，意指前文中提到的地点 the place in Wansheng。例如：This is the house where I once lived. 这就是我曾经住过的房子。

另外，句中的 stretching along the lake shore 为现在分词，作后置定语，

修饰 the mountains。例如：I like the girl standing at the gate. 我喜欢站在门边的那个女孩。

2. Only the nascent buds could be picked as required. 仅取鲜嫩茶芽。

Only... could... 在文中意为"只有……才……"。例如：Only Tom could work out the problem. 只有汤姆才能解决这个问题。

as required 为方式状语从句的省略句，原句为"as it is required"。

3. Known as the King in Bamboo Shoots, the quadrate bamboo shoots stand out in nature and are unique in China. 方竹笋人称笋中之王，世界一绝。

known as 位于句首，作定语，修饰 the quadrate bamboo shoots，来自固定短语 be known as，意为"作为……而出名"。例如：This design came to be known as the oriental style. 这种设计作为东方风格而出名。

stand out 为动词短语，在文中意为"脱颖而出"。例如：Four points stand out as being more important than the rest. 有四点比其余各点更为重要。

4. Since they grow up in unpolluted mountains, only the most delicacy title matches its quality. 出自无污染的大山之中，堪称山珍佳肴。

此句中，since 意为"因为"，引导原因状语从句。例如：Since he asks you, you'll tell him why. 因为他询问了，你就应告诉他为什么。

Translation of the reading texts 课文译文

舌尖上的黑山

黑山以其美景闻名，然而其美食也是一大特色。

黑山红茶

湖岸连绵的茶山，是重庆名茶"滴翠剑名"的产地。每年新茶飘香，以茶会友，客似云来。新知故友，知己同游，领略茶中真趣。

黑山红茶于清明前采自高山深谷，仅取鲜嫩茶芽。观其形，匀整乌润；赏其汤，橙黄透亮；闻其味，馥郁芬芳。

黑山方竹笋干

方竹笋人称笋中之王，世界一绝。中国独有，质嫩肉厚，色美味鲜，出自无污染的大山之中，堪称山珍佳肴。

黑山谷猕猴桃

黑山谷猕猴桃产自海拔 700~1 000 米的黑山山脉，有得天独厚的自然生长环境，无农药，无化肥，是营养健康的果实佳品，吃上一口怀恋永久。

黑山腊味

黑山腊味加工原料选用当地优质猪肉，严格按照 ISO 9001 : 2008 国际质量管理体系把关，咸淡适口，传统风味，是馈赠亲朋好友和宴请宾客的上乘佳品。

黑山的美食不胜枚举，喜爱美食的你心动了吗？

Summary writing　摘要写作

Answer the questions and give a brief introduction to a Bite of Black Valley within 60 words.

1. What makes Black Valleys famous?

2. How many great foods do Black Valley have?

3. What is your favorite food?

Homework　家庭作业

Your pen friend John is interested in the food in Black Valley; you are required to send him an email, briefly introducing the food here to him within 100 words.

Lesson 21   A Bite of Jinqiao

Jinqiao is another good place to meet your taste in Wansheng. Grapefruit, honey, pickles, and dried radish are popular in China.

Jinqiao Grapefruit

The Jinqiao grapefruit, which has thin peel and small core, but tender, refreshing and juicy pulp, is standing out of so many hybrid varieties of grapefruit. Its peel is smooth and shiny. If you have a taste, within its sweetness hides a little bit sour covered with fragrance.

Honey from Wild Flowers

Jinqiao pure honey comes from many sorts of wild flowers growing in deep mountains. It is very nutritious without additives or artificial processing. Premium honey comes in a hard way, so every bite shall be cherished.

Jinqiao Pickles

Hundreds of years of the techniques which are composed of nine times for pick-ling, and nine sessions of processing purely which are completed by hand bring out Jinqiao pickles' fragrance and flavor that could withstand the test of time, like wine.

Jinqiao Dried Radish

The spicy and hot radish is made of organic high-quality radish through dr-ying, salting, desalination, dehydration and flavoring. The hot taste does not irri-tate you because it is balanced by the spicy flavor. After a bite of this crispy dish, a whiff of sweet lingers on your tongue.

（本文图片由重庆红苗文化旅游发展股份有限公司提供）

Words and expressions 生词和短语

grapefruit［ˈɡreɪpfruːt］ *n.* 柚子

pickles［ˈpɪklz］ *n.* 盐菜

hybrid［ˈhaɪbrɪd］ *adj.* 混合的

core［kɔː(r)］ *n.* 核心，果核

pulp［pʌlp］ *n.* 果肉

fragrance［ˈfreɪɡrəns］ *n.* 香味

peel［piːl］ *n.* 皮

nutritious［njuˈtrɪʃəs］ *adj.* 有营养的

artificial [ˌɑːtɪˈfɪʃl] *adj.* 人造的

flavor [fleɪvə(r)] *n.* 滋味，风味

desalination [ˌdiːˌsælɪˈneɪʃn] *n.* 脱盐

dehydration [ˌdiːhaɪˈdreɪʃn] *n.* 脱水

Notes to the texts 课文注解

1. If you have a taste, within its sweetness hides a little bit sour covered with fragrance. 尝上一口，味甜带酸，有香气。

此句中的 with its sweetness hides a little bit sour covered with fragrance. 为完全倒装句，将 within its sweetness 放在句首，谓语 hides 放在主语之前，意在对金桥柚子整体口感做一个强调。例如：Behind the door was locked a man. 一个男人被锁在了门后。

2. Hundreds of years of the techniques which are composed of nine times for pickling, and nine sessions of processing purely which are completed by hand bring out Jinqiao pickles' fragrance and flavor that could withstand the test of time, like wine. 秉承上百年的传统手艺，采取纯手工采收腌制，"九腌九制"，做出来的老盐菜像酒一样，时间越久，味道越醇厚。

hundreds of 意为"成百上千的"，类似的表数量的短语还有 thousands of "成千上万的"，millions of "成百上千万的"等。例如：The exhibition has attracted thousands of visitors. 展览吸引了成千上万的参观者。Lower interest rates pleased millions of mortgage payers. 较低利率使上百万抵押贷款支付人感到高兴。

由 which 引导的两个句子为限制性定语从句，分别修饰 hundreds of years of the techniques 和 nine sessions of processing purely。例如：A shop should keep a stock of those goods which sell best. 商店应存有最畅销的货物。

be composed of 意为 "由……组成"。例如：The force would be composed of troops from NATO countries. 该部队将由北约各国的军队组成。

3. The spicy and hot radish is made of organic high-quality radish through drying, salting, desalination, dehydration and flavoring. 麻辣萝卜干，选用优质绿色生态萝卜为原料，经自然风干、盐渍、脱盐、脱水、拌料而成。

be made of 在文中意为 "由……做成" 与 be made from 意思相近，但 be made of 表达的是做成后能看见原材料，be made from 是做成后看不见原材料。如：The desk is made of wood. 桌子由木材做成（桌子做成后还可以看见木材，所以用 be made of）。These cakes are made from sugar, butter and water. 蛋糕由糖、黄油和水做成（蛋糕做成后看不见糖粉、黄油或者水，所以用 be made from）。

Translation of the reading texts　课文译文

舌尖上的金桥

万盛金桥镇是另一个可以满足你味蕾的好去处。那里的柚子、蜂蜜、盐菜和萝卜干全国畅销。

金桥柚子

柚的杂交品种颇多，金桥柚子因果皮较薄、果心小、果肉细嫩、爽口、多汁而脱颖而出。它的果皮平滑而光亮。尝上一口，味甜带酸，有香气。

野山花蜜

金桥土蜂蜜，由深山多种野花蜜汇聚而成，无添加，无加工，营养价值丰富。好蜜来之不易，且吃且珍惜。

金桥 "老盐菜"

金桥 "老盐菜" 秉承上百年的传统手艺，采取纯手工采收腌制，"九腌九制"，做出来的老盐菜像酒一样，时间越久，味道越醇厚。

金桥萝卜干

麻辣萝卜干，选用优质绿色生态萝卜为原料，经自然风干、盐渍、脱盐、脱水、拌料而成。其口味辣而不燥，麻辣并重，香脆可口，口感回甜。

Summary writing 摘要写作

Answer the questions and briefly introduce one food in Jinqiao within 50 words.

1. How many kinds of food are there in Jinqiao?
2. Which one is your favorite?
3. Which one do you want to recommend to your friend? Why?

Homework 家庭作业

Your friend Lucy plans to visit Wansheng and she writes a letter asking for some information about it. Please collect some videos and texts about Wansheng to share with her.

Afterword
后记

Charming Wansheng（魅力万盛）选修课程，是结合万盛全域旅游特点，按照新课改和《普通高中英语课程标准》（2017 年版，2020 年修订）的要求，根据重庆市英语教育课程改革和关于精品课程建设实施的需要，以及我校英语教学的实际情况和特色，创新建立起来的英语特色校本课程。

编写这套选修教材是我们由来已久的愿望，目的是通过特色化课程的开发和教学实践，以英语为载体共享万盛旅游大餐，在爱家爱国情怀中传承万盛的旅游文化瑰宝，提高学生的文化审美能力和鉴赏能力，加深学生的英语积淀，增强学生的英语功底，提升学生的核心素养。

这套教材是我校校本教材编写组全体成员辛勤努力的成果，是集体智慧的结晶。在本书的成书过程中，编写组成员倾注了大量的时间和精力，他们利用工余时间，精心编撰，反复校对，数易其稿，终于付梓。

我们衷心感谢万盛经济技术开发区管理委员会和教育局等上级

部门对我们的大力支持，感谢重庆红苗文化旅游发展股份有限公司提供的帮助，感谢学校领导对我们的大力支持。

本书在编写过程中参考了大量资料，所收资料庞杂，部分图片选自网络，如有侵权，请立即联系我们。虽然我们在编写过程中反复酝酿、推敲、校对、审核，但百密难免一疏，加上我们水平有限，书中错漏之处在所难免，敬请大家不吝赐教，以使这套校本教材更加完善，谢谢！

重庆市第四十九中学校

英语精品选修课教材编委会